Jewish Lightning

Barry Zack

I0087534

ISBN 978-0-692392-39-3

Published by
Laugh-a-Minute Publications
7157 Rue De Palisades
Sarasota, Fl, 34238

Dedication

My thanks to my beloved wife, Joanne, who has put up with me through thick and thin (mostly thin), and to the people who were inspirations for some of the book's characters and events. They shall remain nameless, in this dedication, but will doubtless recognize themselves upon reading this book.

Chapter 1 • Coming Out Party

"When I was born I was so surprised I didn't talk for a year and a half."

-Gracie Allen

I lay face up, aware of my body, but feel nary a sensation. Walls tinted a garish green rapidly fly past me. Wherever this is, they could sure use a good decorator. A familiar smell hangs in the air. The light seems dim, as though a gauzy membrane has been pulled over my face. Are my eyes blinking, or are those strobe lights flashing rapidly? I'm just not sure. My torso shivers, my teeth chatter, and all this despite the weight of several blankets wrapped around me. I can hear only muffled sounds. I want to reach for my ears to clear any possible obstruction, but I'm unable to move a solitary muscle.

My ears register the sounds of indecipherable words. They become louder and then softer as I zoom through this corridor. The rolling bed upon which my body rests rumbles over bump after bump, bobbing my head up and down. I'm close to a wall that, seen through blurry eyes, has the appearance of textured metal. Now there's the sensation of dropping downward. The motion stops abruptly and I resume forward motion over another bump. "Hey, easy, there's an injured person here," I want to cry out, but the words just won't come.

White coats form a blur around me. My gurney smashes up against a set of doors, flinging them open, making an angry whap as they hit the walls.

"Hey, rough!" I want to say, but cannot. I make out the shrill voice of a woman shouting, "Get him on the table, stat." I think that's what I just heard but can't be certain. I have a burning desire to ask just where I am, but control of my vocal continues to elude me.

"He's lost a lot of blood," I think I just heard, or something equally unsettling.

"Grab his arms and slide him—one…two…three… NOW."

This time it's the voice of a man with a clipped accent that even in my condition I recognize as Hindi or Urdu. I'm good at accents, and I never forget anything I hear, see or smell. But this is unlike me—unable to pinpoint that smell permeating my nostrils or figure out where the fuck I am. I hear the clank of small metal objects, accompanied by electronic beeps.

Red and green lights blink all around, and a gigantic light fixture with a concentric circular lens hovers just above my motionless body. The stark brightness should make me squint, but somehow doesn't. I hear the snapping of elastic from several points around me. There is a loud hum in the background, muffling the sound of a voice calling for thirty cc's of pharmaceutical something. The hiss of my own breath continues in a steadily diminishing volume. My lids are becoming heavy and it's as though they are being pulled shut. I'm experiencing a not unpleasant dizziness. The last thing I remember is telling that big schmuck on the train platform to turn down his fucking boom box.

The voices are gone. Peace. I'm floating on a bed of gossamer. Lighter and lighter… I'm beginning to see something strange, yet somehow familiar.

I'm in a lightless tunnel, having no idea how I got here, or how long I've been here, but it does sort of seem like a lifetime. It is warm and slippery, but not in an unpleasant way. By now, I am quite familiar with the texture of these walls that engulf me. I'm comforted and reassured as I rub up against them. Lately I've been noticing that I fit more snugly within them than when I was first conscious of them.

Irregular vibrations seem to come from all directions at once. There are muffled voices outside my tunnel. My head, pointing in a different direction than before, feels natural, although I can't recall it having ever been thus positioned. The walls, as if alive, form textured ripples that move in the direction of my head. At first these sensations occur intermittently, and then seem more deliberate and continuous. As they gain in strength, so too does the irregular vibration. The ripples seem to clutch my body, taking me with them in their downward motion. This seems far less peaceful than what I'm used to.

Disturbing sounds, growing ever louder, find their way into my closed sanctuary. They are now a multitonal chorus. What has contained my steadily growing infant body, these many months, alternately lifts and falls.

The vibration is steadier and more tremulous than moments ago. I can feel myself in a forward thrust, my head forming a wedge that pushes the tunnel walls apart. The top of my head now is much colder than the rest of me. I am terrified by all of this, and one screaming voice I can hear above the din compounds my fear. There is intense pressure on my head as it inches slowly forward. Warm liquids ooze and squirt out around my face.

My body abruptly stops moving, as if cemented into its position. I hear the buzz of alarmed voices along with shrieks that seem to emanate from outside that chamber in which I lay. I want to return to where it is safe. The ripples have lost some of their power, unable to continue their task of propelling me forward. I lay here exposed, no longer protected by the sanctuary that has preserved and comforted me for as long as I can remember. I detect an icy cold object sliding along the walls, touching my face on both sides. The object is alien to me and its intrusive presence adds to my frightened state. It now grips me, like the walls had done before. My journey forward resumes, even more slowly, begrudgingly.

Suddenly I'm conscious of light, something I had not previously experienced. The screams, moans and groans have stopped. Something tugs at an extension protruding from the middle of my tiny body. There is a snipping sound, freeing me from my connection to the tunnel. Huge hands lift me up and grab my tiny ankles. I helplessly dangle from this giant hand. How could that happen? Suddenly there's a slap on my rear end. Hey, what'd I do? I just got here. Another slap. Now I'm aware of a completely new sensation, as air rushes into my miniature lungs for the first time. I guess I don't like it very much, or I'm mourning the loss of my dignity, because I start to cry for the first time. With this the sounds of applause and laughter fill the room. The odd mixture of hilarity and my wailing does not seem to disturb these people, but I am not all that thrilled about it. I'm suddenly very hungry, even famished, as though I hadn't eaten—as indeed I hadn't.

I have this weird craving for something warm and fleshy. My miniscule lips make sucking motions. Where did I learn that?

Oh, yes, much better. They must be psychic, because before I know it, the very thing I crave, the object of all of my desires, is here before me in its magnificent splendor. I sense a connection between this morsel and the container from which I just emerged. Would they send me back there again later? It would be nice, it would be comforting, but judging from the travail that accompanies my arrival in this new, strange, cold, dry world, I rule out the possibility. Too bad, because I really dug it in there. It was private, fairly quiet, warm and cozy, and best of all, no giant claw scooping me up and smacking my bottom. But this? I don't know. I instinctively bury my face in the soft giving mass, to which I am mysteriously drawn.

I find what I know will provide me with means to satisfy my rapacious hunger.

I suck away at the rubbery protrusion. Harder and harder do I suck, but nary a drop passes to my impatient mouth. At last the warm liquid oozes slowly into me. It tastes odd, but for some reason I expect better. I'm not sure how I know this? Have I ever tasted this stuff before? Still, I suck and suck. Despite the funny taste, I somehow know this is the only sustenance available to me at the moment. Besides, laying on top of this lovely blanket of flesh, my naked body feeling its warmth radiating through me, reminds me a little of being inside the tunnel.

Time passes and I feel a little sick. My belly now aches and this is new for me. When I was inside I never felt pain—a little bouncing around, but never any pain. I don't think these people have this idea fully worked out yet.

I'm lifted up, and abruptly pulled away from my one worldly possession, denying me access to the only thing I really care about. The stuff tasted odd, but it was a living. Someone is holding me and I can feel motion.

There are bizarre smells all around me. I sense that I have been moved to a different location. In this new place, I hear lots of wailing, sort of like the sounds I made when they slapped me on the ass. I decide to join in. Are these other screams the result of similar treatment? What's with these sadistic people? Oh, now what? I'm on my back and I can feel one leg lifted, and then the other while some kind of soft fabric is slid underneath me.

Soft hands touch me in some very private places. You get very little respect around here—that's for sure. They're wiping me and spilling this oily stuff between my legs. Actually, it feels pretty good. I hope they don't stop too soon. They do. Part of the cloth comes from between my chubby little drumsticks and covers me. Now it feels tight, but tolerable.

Boy, am I tired. I'd like to sleep if these other guys would just pipe down.

Gee, I miss my container!

Chapter 2 • Religion on the Cutting Edge

"Why are Jewish boys circumcised? Because Jewish women won't touch anything unless it's ten percent off."

-Unknown

The one with the milk containers holds me tightly in her arms, as if afraid she might drop me. She rocks me in her arms, and between that and the gentle motion of the moving car, I'm lulled into a peaceful sleep.

The next thing I feel is a large pair of hands, slowly lifting me out of Miss Milk Jugs' lap. A loud thud, as the door closes, brings me to a wakeful state.

A very tired little me is carried through a hallway. We stop as I hear metal jiggling and a big door being pushed open. They lay me down in this thing with wooden bars all around it. I just want to go back to sleep, and I do.

I am just beginning to see more than only light patterns, and can now make out some shapes. I'm conscious of one particular person who talks to me constantly. I'm pretty sure it's the one with the strange tasting milk. She talks or hums to me whenever she comes near. I haven't even a vague notion what she's blathering about.

Occasionally others enter my room and examine me from behind the bars that surround my bassinet. I can make out the large shapes of several people who all talk at the same time. I have no idea what they're saying.

They make strange sounds at me. Someone with a deep voice approaches my little bed a few times a day, singing as he lifts me up.

They take turns diapering me. Some are far more adept at it than others. While cleaning up my smelly mess, someone sticks me in my little fanny with a thin, sharp object. I am not shy over my displeasure. Then I have an epiphany! If I need something, all I have to is scream like hell and they will come running.The wailing technique seems to work every time. I can make out that these objects all look gigantic compared to little me, but I sense that I'm running the show. Power! I really appreciate having it.

The milk lady doesn't do the breast thing anymore. She must have become a little tit-shy after those first several episodes. That makes two of us. Something rubbery is stuck into my puckered mouth. It sort of feels a little like a Mommy breast, but I do not fool easily. I think I know a fake nipple when I suck one, but I'm convinced that the milk from this thing is a damn sight better than the original—with all due respect to the person with the tainted milk.

Today, the place is more crowded than usual. I feel almost like I'm back in the nursery with the wailers, again. I was just beginning to become accustomed to the privacy, the invasion of which doesn't exactly please me. I express my displeasure with as much volume as my immature lungs can muster. This shakes everyone up, and they rush in to see what my problem is. Actually, I have very few problems. None of them take more than a few minutes to solve. Feed me; burp me; change me. That's about it. I'm easy.

I admit to being a bit wary of the klutz who stuck me, wishing that the clumsy oaf would learn some diaper pin basics. I do not forget easily, and do hold a grudge.

Hey! Someone's hand is down the front of my diaper and they're probing for something. What they expect to find under there, I cannot imagine, any more than I could imagine anything else. Well, I let out a scream, so they checked out the first logical possibility.

Now "Deep Voice" lifts me and hugs me gently. That very large hand (compared to mine) becomes a cushion for my head. I'm clutched tightly as I'm carried to another part of the room. I somehow sense nervousness all around me, and then it suddenly becomes deadly quiet. I am aware of a new presence in the space. I feel the cold coming off the body of this new arrival as it approaches me. There is a very low volume of muttering and whispering. Why do they bother to whisper? I don't understand a damn word, anyway.

The cloth protecting my nether regions is removed. I can't imagine why? I'm neither wet nor soiled. I'm totally confused. I hear noises reminding me of the day I first popped out of the tunnel—sort of like the clanking of metal objects. The smell is also familiar. Then there is a new odor—and more clanking, but different from before.

The strange man begins to chant, making sounds unlike anything I'd heard during my eight day stay in this new world. The voice is not exactly melodic. I peer through glassy, barely opened eyes in an attempt to make out the stranger's shape, as its upper body moves back and forth. More chanting, louder chanting and then even stranger body movements ensue.

An aroma with which I have no familiarity becomes stronger and seems to move from where the chanter stands to where that diaper used to be. I feel my thing being rubbed with that smelly stuff. Then another aroma nears my face. They're making me taste it? It's awful, I think.

The singsong continues. There is not another sound in the room except for the guy with the weird body movements. Does this guy realize he might be disturbing others? He is certainly doing little for my tranquility.

"OWWWWW," I scream, after a sharp pain in a very inconvenient place. I display my absolute abhorrence with an outburst that drowns out the singer. I violently kick my legs up and down, and wave my hands frantically in the air. The room fills with applause, laughter and loud mumbling, while an 8-day-old, who did not ask to be here, is filled with pain, not to mention embarrassment. These are some weird people. I wonder what other delights are in store for me next?

There is more laughter, then the pouring of some smelly beverage, and the clinking of glasses. But to my relief, there's no more singing from the guy with the dancing head. I just want to sleep. My thumb enters my mouth. Pretending it's a nipple, I suck on it while my forefinger makes circles around my tiny nose. My head feels heavy as I pass out.

Chapter 3 • C'mon Baby Light My Fire

"How is it that one match can start a forest fire, but it takes a whole box of matches to start a campfire?"

-Christy Whitehead

It's a typical Friday night—the Jewish Sabbath, or *Shabbas* to us. Mommy has completed the Sabbath candle lighting ritual in the kitchen. Sol chimes in with "*Mazel Tov*" and "*Au Mein*," two of the few ethnic expressions he ever utters.

What does candle lighting have to do with Chinese food, I wonder, confusing *Au Mein* with *Lo Mein*.

"It's not appropriate, Sol," she chastises him. "You don't say either of those things when *Shabbas* candles are lit on the Sabbath."

Sol looks down and seems embarrassed. He knows or cares little about religion, but loves the idea of being Jewish, and its traditions. He was never quite sure why Mommy lit candles on *Shabbas*—and I certainly have no clue.

When I ask her to explain what purpose they serve, Mommy tells me, "To remember the passing of Uncle Chatzkil," a name, like so many of Eastern European origin, could drown out the candles with spittle when spoken. Chatzkil, after whom I am named, was her father's uncle. He died falling off the rear of a moving trolley car on which he was attempting to hitch a free ride. This was something children often did in Brooklyn, but it was highly unusual for a man of seventy to attempt it. Mommy confuses *Yahrzeit* candles with *Shabbas* candles, but what else is new?

I learned that these candles must be lit before the sun goes down, or God becomes furious. It's only one of the many things He gets upset about, as I had learned in my first few sessions at yeshiva nursery school.

Observing that the sun has already set, I conclude that my mother will probably be punished. "Will she have to stand in a corner?" I wonder, "like Rabbi Schmuel makes me do when something I've done displeases him?"

I've been noticing that Mommy's belly is looking bigger and bigger each day, and I am thinking that God might have dispensed His justice by making her fat.

Daddy reaches for the radio to turn it on. The opera, live from the *Metropolitan*, is about to be broadcast.

"No, Sol," Mommy shrieks, blocking his hand from touching the dial.

"You know we don't listen to the opera on *Shabbas*."

I am so curious about all these rules God has set up that He expects us all to follow. Sol withdraws his hand, giving in to the Edie edict.

Mommy warns me, once again, not to go near the candles because I might burn myself. This plants the seed of curiosity, and I think about the ways I could learn exactly what "burning yourself" feels like. Does God punish you with fire? I must find out.

Daddy goes into the next room to work on his stamp collection. I surmise that God must also collect stamps, because Mommy makes no attempt to stop Daddy from this pursuit, EVEN THOUGH IT IS *SHABBAS*.

I follow Daddy into the living room, and take a seat opposite him at the bridge table, where I expect to see at least a million stamps laid out. Daddy opens one of many books he told me are called stamp albums. He licks a bonding sticker, puts it on the back of a stamp, and affixes it to a page in the album. Daddy tells me that the stamp he has just pasted in is from Somaliland, exclaiming, "Isn't that a beauty?"

He follows that up with a promise that one day, this stamp collection will be mine. I am confused as to how that will happen.

Water runs in the kitchen sink so that Mommy can finish doing the dishes. It takes her quite a while to scrub a pot because, as usual, she burned whatever it was that she cooked. Mommy does not have a light touch in the kitchen, but I am too unsophisticated to know the difference between something cooked and a burnt offering. Daddy is shy about openly criticizing her cooking, or anything else she does, for that matter.

"Would it kill you to help me with the dishes once in a while, Sol?" speaks her agitated voice. "In my condition, I shouldn't have to stand on my feet so much."

Daddy grins, and looks at me, quietly whispering, "Maybe if she didn't use a blow torch when she cooks, cleaning up would be easier."

"Did you say something, Sol? Because if you don't like my cooking…"

I am fascinated by just how she could have heard his comment over the din of running water; so is Daddy.

"Coming right in," he dutifully replies, leaving me alone with Somaliland and the rest of Africa.

After Daddy completes the "volunteer" task of scrubbing the unscrubbable, muttering under his breath during the painful ordeal, Mommy informs her family that *Fibber, McGee and Molly* is about to come on the radio. God apparently excludes this show from the *Shabbas* taboo.

Mommy often displays mood swings since becoming pregnant and she sometimes takes the form of a controlling martinet. Our family listens to that show each week, which usually begins with a cacophony caused by a pile of junk falling down from a closet shelf, sending the radio and live audience into fits of laughter, and brings a look of bewilderment on my face.

While they sit back and enjoy the frivolity—which I fail to appreciate—I wander back into the kitchen; my absence goes unnoticed.

I locate the two glass candleholders, their contents flickering in an otherwise darkened room. Mommy moved them to a shelf that, supposedly, I can't reach. I stealthily slide a chair in place, and shove a phone book atop it, providing me with the altitude to not only see the candles, but also to wave my hand over them and feel their heat. I am extra careful not to place my fingers too close to the flame, not knowing just what God might have up his sleeve.

After several flicker-filled minutes, I become bored with the experience and want to liven things up. I ignore a voice in my head that is uttering words of discouragement. An empty candy wrapper had been left on the counter, which I grab, drawing it over one of the candles. Within seconds it ignites, flaring up in my hand.

"Ow!" I yell, quickly dropping the burning cellophane. I watch it flutter down, landing on a pile of newspapers in the corner of the room. I can still remember the headline on page one:

Dr. Einstein Dead At 76

I don't concern myself too much with Einstein, thinking I might be following close behind.

"Do you smell something, Sol?" I can hear Mommy ask from the next room.

"No," my Dad replies, having become inured to unpleasant aromas emanating from the kitchen, for purely defensive reasons.

"I smell smoke, Sol," comes as an alarmed and elevated shriek.

Both parents rush to the kitchen simultaneously, almost knocking each other over in the doorway. They observe their mischievous child's attempt at drowning the burning pile of newsprint in water from the sink, one glass at a time. Three Katzes cough and choke as smoke fills the tiny kitchen.

Daddy, thinking quickly, lifts the burning pile of papers and drops it into the sink, while Mommy rushes to open the window to let out the smoke. It takes several minutes for the running water to extinguish the flames, while a chorus of cries and squeals fills the room.

God was sure quick to notice what I did, I think. "Maybe I shouldn't underestimate Him in the future!" I posit. The next several minutes consist of Mommy and Daddy fanning the smoke out the window while showing their displeasure with mischievous me. This is followed by the sound of fire engine sirens becoming louder and louder.

The wailing abruptly ceases, and not a minute later, comes a pounding on our door. Daddy runs to open it, and is met by a group of men in big funny hats and rain slickers, led by a gigantic fellow holding the biggest axe I have ever seen.

Chapter 4 • Strangers on a Train

"One touch of nature makes the whole world kin."

-William Shakespeare

Mommy and Daddy no longer talk about what was supposed to be a new brother or sister for me. She also does not look as fat as she did a few months ago. When I ask about what happened to the baby she was supposed to have, she tells me that God was not yet ready for that to happen. God changes his mind easily, I conclude.

My mother refers to herself as "Mommy" when communicating with me. That's what I call her, even though others use different names. When I try calling her "Honey" like Daddy does, she says, "I'm Mommy, not Honey. Only your Daddy calls me Honey."

This is thoroughly confusing, especially since her friends called her "Edie," and the man at the butcher shop refers to her as "Mrs. Katz."

Mommy has been preparing for this day for quite a while—in fact since my last birthday, when I turned five. I know that because there were five lit blue candles on the cake, which I was encouraged to blow out. She has been promising me how much fun we'll all have when summer arrives. I have no concept of summer, or any other season for that matter. But summer is a funny word. "Summer, summer," I repeat, giggling each time. But it does sound like I might enjoy it. I try to picture sand and waves, and vaguely remember seeing a beach in a book my aunt Chalya gave me.

Mommy dresses me in short pants which she calls a bathing suit, overlaid with a sailor's outfit, complete with white cap. She suggests that I go to the mirror and see how cute I look. I don't understand the meaning of cute, but do enjoy seeing my reflection and funny faces peering back at me. This continues to be an important source of entertainment for me, seeing just how silly I can make that face in the mirror look.

Mommy is expecting her friend Jeanne to come by shortly, and then we can all head off to the beach. I wait, not-so-patiently, for the doorbell to ring while clutching a pail and shovel, uncertain how these implements will be used. I have been assured that they will provide a most enjoyable experience.

At last, the doorbell rings. Food prepared in advance is gathered and we are off.

After a two block walk we reach the subway. Mommy deposits a nickel in a slot to activate what she explains is a turnstile. I am then invited to walk ahead under this device, and Mommy follows right behind. Jeanne makes a similar deposit and manages to squeeze her rotund body through what for her is a narrow opening.

We wait inside the station for our train to arrive. I notice that when I speak in a loud voice, I hear what Mommy explains is an echo. This is so exciting that I feel encouraged to yell even louder, to the chagrin of other waiting passengers, including Jeanne.

At last, a gigantic object, which Mommy identifies as "the train," emerges from the tunnel connected to the station, making a deafening noise before coming to a stop. Mommy nudges me into the subway car, already filled with other people similarly dressed and carrying things one might bring to a beach.

Jeanne takes up almost two full seats on the train. I stand on a seat covered in woven cane and stare out the window, my nose nudged up against it. There is not much to see, except for the dark and dingy walls outside the glass.

Soon everything brightens as the train emerges from the tunnel and is now traveling on tracks in the open air. I'm very excited as the Brighton bound train clickety-clacks past one station after another. I ask Mommy why our train is not stopping at these stations, and she explains that this is an express, which will make only a few stops before arriving at our destination.

I can't stop staring at a man they call "the conductor," who wears a funny hat and the longest keychain I've ever seen. I am fascinated when the buttons are pressed, and then, as if by magic, doors fly open. The uniformed man announces, "Last stop. Brighton Beach. Last stop. No more passengers."

Mommy grabs my hand and leads me off the train, down a long flight of stairs onto the street. I look up at the elevated station from which we have just descended, and I am in awe of the slew of tracks, wires and lights seen from our vantage point on the street.

We now begin what seems like a long march to the beach. With me tightly grasped in her arms, Mommy and her friend trudge up a flight of stairs to what is introduced to me as "the boardwalk." She deposits me on the ancient wooden boards with a warning not to remove my shoes or I will get splinters in my feet. I have no concept of a splinter, but her tone is ominous enough to convince me to heed the warning, which is always difficult for me. I love taking off my shoes as well as the rest of my clothing. We proceed across the planks to the far side of the boardwalk, and then it is revealed—in all its splendor, a wide span of sand stretching as far as my eyes can see in either direction. Even more dazzling, a bluish-black ocean, looking as though it must drain off where it meets the horizon, and grayish white wisps where the water hits the shore.

Birds are everywhere and the air fills with their shrill calls. Mommy informs me that those are seagulls. This confuses me because they bear no resemblance to the Siegel family that lives in the apartment down the hall. They made their own loud noises, sounding nothing like these birds.

Jeanne and Mommy argue as to where on the vast beach their blanket should be laid down. It has to be far enough from the water's edge to prevent their stuff from drowning in an unexpected wave, but not too far from the shore, because Jeanne hates walking any more than necessary.

After much deliberation, a spot on the sand is selected for us to settle.

Mommy rolls down my sailor hat so that the brim can protect my eyes from the strong sun. She strips me down to my bathing suit and encourages me to remove my shoes. I gleefully oblige. She and Jeanne remove their street clothes and neatly fold them before dropping them on their blanket. The two women are contrasts in body types. Mommy is much thinner than she was before God changed his mind, but not exactly slender. Though compared to Jeanne, she reminds me of that girl in the *Popeye* cartoon.

Mommy takes my hand and leads me toward the surf. I am unconvinced of the safety in doing this. She tries to assure me that she will not let anything bad happen to me. I reluctantly follow her, or more accurately, allow her to drag me. We stand on a spot where the sand is wet and firm.

Little ripples of water tickle my toes. I can hear waves crashing a few feet from where I'm standing, and it makes me want to return to the safety of our blanket.

"No, I don't want to go in the water, Mommy," I shriek, but she is persistent, for which I am ultimately grateful. After waves that rise only to Mommy's knees, but seem gigantic from my perspective, knock me down several times, I begin to enjoy the experience. This is a lot more fun than a bath, I think, except for this annoying bathing suit, which acts like a sand magnet. I try pulling it down, but my mother, observing the rules of decorum, whatever that means, prevents me from doing so. I wonder exactly where those rules are written down.

After lunch, where I learn the true meaning of the word "sandwich," I ask Mommy if I can go back in the water. She tells me what every Jewish mother informs her child after consuming food at the beach, "You have to wait at least a half an hour, or you will get terrible cramps."

I am unable to judge how long a half hour actually is, and after a few seconds I again ask her if I can go in the water, now. This happens repeatedly, until she has either given up, or the time has actually elapsed.

Later that day, after I've built what Mommy called the best sand castle she'd ever seen, I'm told that it's time to go home. I don't greet this as good news, since there is still quite a bit more sand left on the beach for me to construct additional architectural splendors. I indicate my displeasure by screaming the entire time as we head back to the train station.

Jeanne walks behind us and pretends not to be part of our group, all the while holding her ears—not an easy feat when carrying bags of towels and a blanket. When we arrive back at the station my crying ceases, because I ran out of tears, or at least crocodile ones. Mommy seems to appreciate the silence, while Jeanne, trudging at a snail's pace, is nowhere in sight. Mommy realizes that she has no more nickels to put in the box that permits entry through the turnstile.

"Stay here, Henry," she says, leaving me in front of the turnstile while she walks up to the man behind a window, paper money waving in her hand.

The height of the turnstile is no obstacle for me, so I just walk on through. Soon I am out on the platform as a big train rumbles into the Brighton Beach Station, its horn wailing as it rounds the turn. It looks to me exactly like the one that brought us to Brighton. It even has the same number on the side of the car, 7E13314. I remember things like that, but can't explain why.

Despite a tiny voice in my head suggesting that this might not be a good idea, I decide to save time and board as soon as I observe the doors opening. Others passengers follow and the train soon fills with beach-attired people, none of whom seem at all familiar to me. I looked around for Mommy or Jeanne and can spot neither. I watch in trepidation as the train doors close, while from the distance I can hear Mommy screaming, "HENRY…"

.

Chapter 5 • Bad Aunt Chalya

Frankie and Johnny were sweethearts,
Boy, how they could love!
Swore to be true to each other,
True as the stars above!
'Cause he was her man,
But he done her wrong!

-"Frankie and Johnny" by Hughie Cannon

Aunt Chalya is my mother's cousin. Whenever I try to utter her name I have difficulty pronouncing it without spitting all over myself. That "chhha" sound, familiar in so many *Yiddish* words, is the culprit. Chalya came to America from Poland after the war. My mother told me that my aunt joined the hoards of others who arrived in New York after surviving the Holocaust. I didn't know what that word meant, and was sure my mother was mispronouncing it.

Whenever Mommy spoke with any of these refugee relatives, the conversation would be interlaced with *Yiddish*.

Hardly a sentence was uttered that lacked one of these "Jewish" words. I learned some of this *Yiddish*, overhearing Mommy when she spoke with these refugees she referred to as "Greenies." Whenever she needs to keep me from hearing something "inappropriate" she uses *Yiddish* substitutes for words less suitable for my young ears. It didn't take a genius to figure out which words were "jewfemized."

Chalya never married. According to conversations I overheard, she had little trouble meeting men in the Old Country, but was not very successful in keeping them. Although much of the talk between my mother and Aunt Chalya was difficult to decipher, those *Yiddishisms* constantly getting in the way, I was able to figure out many of them on my own.

When ever Mommy caught me eavesdropping, she urged Chalya to hush up. "Chalya, shush," she would whisper. "The child is listening."

Chalya doesn't speak of this much anymore, but every once in a while, Gershon, her former boyfriend, does come up in conversation. He was her man, but he was doing her wrong—however little that meant to me.

After Chayla leaves our apartment, I asked my mother for an explanation.

"None of your business," she says, but when I pursue it she snaps, "Go ask your father," never suspecting that my Dad would actually tell me. Daddy is uncomfortable discussing boy-girl stuff, especially with a young tyke like me, but he mentions that Chalya's boyfriend was not truthful with her concerning his marital status. This engenders even more questions, until my father finally informs me of poor Aunt Chalya's unrealized wedding plans. He also lets me know how she got her revenge.

It seems Gershon was taking a bath, thinking that he was alone. Chalya had just learned, from a trusted source, about her boyfriend's deception. She tiptoed into the bathroom with a large pot of scalding chicken soup she held by its handles, so heavy she could barely lift it without grunting. Just as Gershon turned around, as he felt a cold draft on his back, resulting from her opening the door, Chalya dumped the entire bucket into the tub—specifically aiming for his lap.

"You're always raving about my chicken soup," she screamed. "Enjoy!"

Gershon was never the same after that, and after hearing that story, neither was I. All this happened before the Nazi takeover of Poland, so her spinsterhood was certainly not the worst of her suffering. I have often been told that very bad things happened to Jews in her country, but Mommy, knowing how upsetting this information could be to a young child, spares me the gory details.

Chalya is big in the local chapter of *Hadassah*, the women's Zionist organization. In addition to all her other responsibilities, she has just volunteered to prepare a dinner for *Hadassah* guests. A trip to the market is required and, lucky me, I get dragged along.

So far, it has been an annoying but eventless experience at the local

A&P. We go from aisle to aisle, as she picks up a piece of fruit here, a carrot bunch there, announcing dissatisfaction over the poor condition of each comestible.

"This one looks like it was picked before the war," she declares, discarding it as if it were stricken with leprosy. Chalya asks me to comment, as if I'm some kind of vegetable guru. She forgets that in the Katz household, food quality is not an issue, mainly because it doesn't exist. I must have used a poor choice of words in one of my responses, which is quickly corrected for imprecise grammar. Though foreign born, she has mastered English quite proficiently, and hopes her influence will aid me in doing the same.

We are in a new section of the market, where poultry is displayed openly. This enables the customer to examine a bird, instead of having to accept the questionable advice of Herman the butcher, who has recently been informed that his services will no longer be required at the Great Atlantic and Pacific Tea Company.

Chayla is surely taking her time giving this chicken the onceover—actually more like a thrice-over. In addition to a visual inspection, she employs the nose test.

"Very important," she states emphatically. "The nose knows. And if the nose says 'no,' I say no."

Suddenly, with the mastery of a great prestidigitator, she makes the bird disappear. I watch Chalya's face as it glances furtively around the aisle for trouble-making eyewitnesses. When she is satisfied that there are none, she stuffs the chicken into her dress, comforted that her larceny is undetected.

I can hardly believe what I know I have just seen (the eyes eye what the eyes eye). Maybe she's figured out a better way to carry the bird though the store, and needs not to be hobbled by one of those pesky, bumpy shopping carts, I assume.

As we approach the checkout counter, my nine-year-old voice queries, "What about the chicken, Aunt Chalya?"

"What chicken, Henry? Where do you see a chicken? The boy has such an imagination," she says as we make our way toward the exit.

When she's confident that we are safely outside the store, with the pur-loined fowl tucked precariously beneath her ponderous bosom, she berates me in a most humiliating manner. I feel the disapproving gaze of every eye on bustling DeKalb Avenue.

"You think, from a store, I would steal a chicken?" she screams in her thickest Eastern European accent. "You embarrassed me so. I'm never tak-ing you…"

The admonishment is immediately interrupted by a quickly approaching man in blue, his badge gleaming in the noonday sunlight. The store man-ager points at her accusingly.

"What've ya got under yer coat, there, miss?" inquires the policeman, with the word "Shannon" on his badge.

"What could I have? As you can see I am a well-endowed woman. This is all me."

"Why don't you open yer coat just to satisfy my curiosity. I'd hate to have to take an innocent woman to the station house for a closer inspec-tion."

The jig is up. There is no way to explain the third copious breast.

We spend the remainder of the day at the 79th precinct, Chalya's epithets spewing in a non-ending stream, reminding me that I am her ruination, not to mention, a *Hadassah* nemesis.

Chapter 6 • Rope Jumping Interuptus

"First you find a little thread, a little thread leads you to a string, and the string leads you to a rope. And from the rope you hang by the neck."

-A. I. Bezzerides

I exit the heavy wrought iron and glass doors of my family's apartment building and emerge onto the sunlit street. Glancing out from under the green canopy adorning the building front, I look to see if the girl of my dreams is anywhere in view. It has been pointed out, by several of my male friends, that my interest in girls is not normal for a healthy twelve-year-old lad. Boys my age rarely show interest in the opposite sex; I seem to be an exception.

Just across the street, on the shady side of Willoughby Avenue, in front of #698, I spot her. Mary Anne O'Shaughnessy skips rope with a few of her friends, including an exotic Middle Eastern looking girl I hadn't noticed before today.

Despite a lively stickball game my pals are playing in the street directly in front of me, my eyes are diverted elsewhere. They are glued on the object of my affection, as I catch glimpses of her white underpants, which teasingly appear with each rise and fall of her little plaid skirt.

She is clad in the uniform of *St. Theresa Girls'* parochial school: a white blouse and aforementioned skirt. The words "E**h**m my name is M**h**ary and my m**h**other's name is M**h**amie…" are breathily parsed from her perfect Irish lips.

Mary Anne is forbidden fruit, especially for boys whose foreskins have been altered in the Hebraic ritual. Her mother doesn't look kindly toward members of my tribe wooing her daughter. The Irish are not much different from my own, or any other ethnic group. We call them *Micks*—part of the more inclusive *Goyim* family; they refer to us as "*Heebs*."

The other girl, whose name I still don't know, keeps looking in my direction. Her hair is black, and very long, descending way below her shoulders. Her eyes are dark and mysterious, and her skin appears deeply tanned, although summer is months away. When I spot her staring she abruptly turns away.

"Hank, over here," shouts Arnie Gold, a neighborhood youth whose body is shaped like a shmoo. He clutches the pink *spaldeen* ball, as if his survival depends upon it. They need a player to fill in for Jerome, forced to leave the game suddenly, after an unfortunate collision with a garbage can while running to catch a pop foul ball. The can was adjudicated to be free of blame in the accident.

Mr. Vaslo, the slovenly building superintendant, shows his displeasure at the event's unfolding, not because Jerome is bleeding profusely from several places, but that he will now be forced to interrupt his busy schedule to shovel the spilled contents back into the fallen can, and right it. This is done without sparing the utterance of several Anglo-Saxon words, interspersed with verbiage in his native tongue, which we neighborhood kids believe to be Martian.

I weigh the consequences of missing the rope skipping entertainment to participate in the stickball game—something that would be a no-brainer for a typical kid.

Only a week earlier, my attention was drawn to a similar leg exposé when I should have been concentrating on a baseball card trade. It was during this inexcusable absence of judgment and a failure to heed the warnings of a hidden voice that advised me otherwise, whereupon I managed to trade away my Whitey Ford (#16), a potential hall of famer, for a Johnny Blanchard (#38).

When my amigos spotted this pitifully dumb act, they pelted me with epithets, questioning my masculinity. After mentally comparing these two players' stats I retained in my memory, I might have joined that chorus.

So, I reluctantly decide in favor of stickball, only because I dread the guys calling me a "sissy."

Street stickball is played in almost every residential neighborhood in the city. Bronzed sewer covers serve as home plate and second base. A third sewer is used to mark the end of the outfield. I walk toward that marker, to occupy the outfielder position, never taking my eyes off the lovely Mary Anne. There will be a definite problem if a ball is hit in my direction, as I have not yet mastered the art of simultaneous ogling and ball catching.

The game, played on the black asphalt of a busy street, is constantly interrupted by passing cars or trucks. The kids are used to it, having learned to quickly fold in between parked cars until the vehicle or vehicles pass, allowing the game to resume. As fielders, our backs face oncoming traffic, and only the catcher, standing behind home sewer, can see these rude interruptions when they occur. In addition to catching each pitched ball that gets past the batter's stick, or chasing after it if he drops it, his job is to shout "**CAR**" when one comes into view, to warn his teammates.

A more powerful voice than Arnold Gold's would be optimal, if a fielder two sewers away could benefit from the warning. With Arnie as catcher, the sudden, unexpected, exceptionally loud outburst of a taxi horn, scaring the be-Jesus out of me, is my only caveat, blaring as I move slowly backwards to catch a well hit fly ball. Needless to say, this does not enhance the ball-catching experience, and explains a sudden wetness in my crotch area. It seems that "be-Jesus" and bodily fluids can be used interchangeably.

I am pissed, literally and figuratively, and can still remember the license plate, "TN4421," on that '54 Checker cab.

My team insists on a "do over" due to the interfering taxicab. The opposing side challenges, claiming that Arnie should have warned his pitcher to wait for the oncoming car to pass before launching the ball. The dispute is not resolved and my team walks off the "field." For this I am eternally grateful, because all I want to do is be back in my apartment, and get out of my soiled underwear and pants. It is also best that Maid Mary Anne doesn't detect the wet stain on my clothing, as that would be an embarrassment I could never live down.

That hope is unrealized, however, as several of the players from the "enemy" team point to my wet spot and this Mary Anne can't fail to notice.

Chapter 7 • Body in the Street

On the sidewalk, one Sunday mornin'
Lies a body oozin' life
Someone's sneaking 'round the corner
Could that someone, perhaps, perchance,
be Mack the Knife?

-The Ballad of Mack the Knife
by Kurt Weill and Bertold Brecht

Our family is on its way home from another trip to the mountains, all of us weary from the seemingly never-ending ride. Dad's driving style makes the trip longer than necessary, his toll-avoidance and his maintaining a pace that would lose a race with a tortoise fighting a leg cramp. Mom has been ripping into him for the last two hours, admonishing him for some of the navigation choices he routinely makes, and for being the slowest driver on the planet.

I am sitting up front with Dad, playing Geography to pass the time.

"Halifax," My father says, thinking that he can stump me, as I try to think of a place beginning with the letter "X."

He is surprised as I come up with Xayabury, a city in French Indochina. I know this because Dad has stamps from all over the world, and happened to show me one from that particular Asian territory. At the time it made me curious, so I read up about it in our World Book Encyclopedia. When I came across Xayabury, I knew it would come in handy some day, because we always play this game during our tedious drives. Plus, the word ends in"Y" which I think might be a challenge for my Pop.

Dad quickly dispels that notion by coming back with "Yately."

"Yately?" I incredulously ask. "Did you just make that up?"

"No," says Dad, confidently, "it's a city in England."

The game continues until I finally became bored, and the passengers in the back seat are sick of hearing us. "Put the radio on, Sol," comes a command from the rear admiral.

"Put the radio on, Sol, PLEASE," Dad retorts.

"Just put the *farkakta* radio on, Sol." This adjective is often used when the speaker is disgusted, which, in Mom's case, is always.

He obediently turns on the radio and the dulcet but unappreciated voice of Maria Callas fills the space.

"Not that, Sol," complains Edie, "Put on something we can all listen to."

"That's Callas. Who could fail to enjoy one of the greatest sopranos of our time?" he asks this musically sophisticated group.

"Put on WNEW," instructs Edie. "At least then we might be able to hear Julius La Rosa or Frank."

"How about WINS 1010?" I suggest. I am only beginning to appreciate this new music called Rock 'n Roll.

To make it fair, they agree to change the station every fifteen minutes so that no one will be driven crazy, not that it would be a very long drive. Sydney, peacefully asleep in her Mommy's lap, mercifully does not weigh in.

As our Pontiac Wagon approaches the George Washington Bridge, I observe the fuel indicator pointing toward "E." Unfortunately I also notice that we've passed the last gas station before the bridge. I was keeping track in my head, and remember that we passed twenty-three gas stations since the start of our trip. I also know how much each one charges for a gallon.

"Dad, looks like we're low on gas," I shout, pointing to the gauge.

"*Oy, Gevalt*," he exclaims, which is Dad's way of saying, "Oh, shit."

"What's happening up there, Sol?" His wife asks, having noticed the panic in his voice.

"Nothing to worry about, Edie. We'll find a gas station after we cross the bridge."

"On a Sunday night, you expect to find gas in the city?"

"We'll find, we'll find, don't worry."

"Don't worry? You couldn't get gas on Route 17? There were a million stations."

Edie's gas station count might be slightly exaggerated, but she's correct that Route 17 would have been a better choice than what is now available.

We drive off the exit ramp and onto the streets of Upper Manhattan, AKA Harlem. Mom is none too pleased as she realizes we are highly outnumbered by people whose complexions are considerably darker than ours. She repeats the *Yiddish* epithet *Shvartzes*, as she pictures our entire family being devoured by cannibals. This comes from a liberal Jew, who reads the *New York Post*, and always votes Democratic!

At Broadway and 166th Street the car begins to sputter, as our gas becomes exhausted.

"You couldn't stop on 17 for gas? You couldn't get gas at the Red Apple Rest? How could you do this to us, Sol?"

We are stopped in the middle of a busy thoroughfare. Dad exits the car and asks me to help him push it towards the curb. My preadolescent body is not much help, and the car rolls at the pace of an injured snail, while drivers behind our vehicle honk with displeasure.

An older Negro man spots us, and approaches the car. Mom looks like she's about to die. Her fears prove unjustified (what else is new?), as the dark-skinned gentleman asks us if he can be of help.

After the problem is explained, Dad, who doesn't share his wife's prejudices, is relieved to learn that there is an open gas station around the corner. The man then helps him push the car to a less obstructive spot near the curb. The paranoid woman in the back seat promptly ensures that all the doors are locked. This doesn't go unnoticed by the Samaritan who has taken time out from whatever he is doing to help fellow humans in distress.

Ten minutes elapse, but to Mom, it is an eternity. Dad reappears, toting a red gasoline can—a weak smile upon his face. He pours the gallon into the tank and drives back over to the station for a fill-up. He is unhappy that gas is considerably pricier in this location than it would have been on Route 17. I can vouch for that. Twenty-one cents per gallon is a lot better than twenty-four.

Dad moves the dusty old Pontiac toward our block, scanning for a place to park. He spots one about a block and a half from our address. As he backs in, despite covering our ears to prevent auditory damage, we can all hear Mom scream, "Sol, we're a hundred miles from our building. In Europe, this man parks."

"It's late, Edie, so we'd better park now, or risk not finding any spot at all." This is an expected response from the guy who might have actually invented the notion of scarcity.

We all grab packages and suitcases from the rear of the vehicle, and start walking. Sydney has the tough burden of having to carry two dolls. The rest of us struggle with an obscene amount of stuff brought on a three day weekend vacation. We get about half of it, knowing a return trip to collect the rest will be required.

Mom continues to complain with every step, and may win a place in the *Guinness Book of Records* 'bitch and moan' category.

Everyone is feeling pretty drained, but we inch forward. I think about how nice a bathroom would be right about now. Then it occurs to me that everyone will want to use the one toilet in our apartment at the same time. This prompts me to ask Dad for the house key, because I can walk pretty fast, especially when I'm motivated.

Dad, known for his dazzling walking speed, unlike his driving, says, "I'll walk with you, Son. I have to go, too."

"Sol, you're not leaving Sydney and me here on a deserted street in the middle of the night."

Dad, lacking support for a fast trek to our building, capitulates, handing me the key. I grab it from his hand before he has a chance to change his mind, or for my mother to change it for him.

"Thanks, Dad," I say as I dart off as fast a kid carrying two suitcases can muster.

When I arrive on our block, I can't fail to notice the police barricades blocking the street from vehicular traffic. Patrol car lights flash and sirens can be heard from arriving additional police vehicles and an ambulance.

As it turns out, a hearse would have been a better choice. As I get closer to our apartment building I observe a large crowd gathered, some of which are wearing the uniform of the local constabulary. They stand in front of Field's Candy Store, surrounding the body of a teenage boy on the blood-soaked pavement. A knife protrudes from a wound right below his ribcage.

Anguished people, standing in front of the entrance to our building, point toward the victim—shaking their heads. I push past them and make it into our bathroom without a moment to spare.

Soon after, my family arrives home. There is serious contention for the only sanitary facility in the apartment. Sydney no longer cares, having wet herself early in the walk from the car. Mom and Dad settle the dispute in the usual manner: he gives in. Dad hopes that this will not be one of Edie's lengthier lavatory processes. He paces outside the bathroom regretting that last cup of coffee he couldn't resist at the Red Apple Rest.

Finally, after all bladders and other organs are relieved, the parents discuss the frightening event that happened outside our building's front door.

"We can't stay in this neighborhood, Sol," declares Mom. "The children and I won't feel safe."

"But, Edie," he protests. "It's one incident. This is a safe neighborhood."

"I'm not living in a place where bodies litter the streets."

"One body," he contends. "You always exaggerate."

I imagine my father adding up numbers is his head, for the costs associated with moving—Jack Benny logic dominating his thinking.

"We're all tired, Edie. Why don't we discuss this in the morning?"

"Uh huh," replies Edie, her fingers poking through the classified section of the newspaper.

Chapter 8 • School Daze

"The authority of those who teach is often an obstacle to those who want to learn."

-Marcus Tullius Cicero

It's the first day in the new school. I had begged my mother not to move in the middle of a school year, but did she listen? So with only a week before summer recess, I find myself, a total stranger in a place where everyone seems to know everyone, except, of course, me.

A woman from the Principal's office escorts me to my room. There are two sixth grade classes at PS 161, and I'm hoping that in my assigned class I'll appreciate the teacher, and she'll like me. This would be a rare occurrence, based on previous experience. I'm assuming it will be a female, because all my teachers at my previous school were ladies (or at least women).

My escort taps gently on the frosted glass panel of the door. A tall and slender female, around thirty, opens it to let me in.

"Good morning, Mr. Katz," she calls out to me, smiling. "We've been expecting you. I'm Mrs. Lee."

I look up at this woman and I'm shocked at how pretty she is, bearing no resemblance to the teachers at PS 25. Even though I'm barely twelve (going on eighteen), I'm beginning to notice differences between the genders that weren't obvious before.

"Gggood mmmorning," I nervously stutter.

"Class," she announces with elevated volume, "let's welcome our newest classmate, Henry Katz."

"Good morning, Henry," they shout in unison.

"Could you call me Hank? My friends all call me Hank," I request, after regaining my composure.

"Good morning, Hank," they shout, respecting my wishes. "And close your zipper," one female classmate adds.

I look down to confirm what I now know is my first blunder at the new school. I forgot to zip up after my last wizz. To think I've been walking around that way for an hour. I guess my mother was too busy to give me a pre-new-school final inspection that would have obviated this gross embarrassment. I correct the problem amid hysterical laughter from the room. Even Mrs. Lee can't keep a straight face.

The seats are assigned according to the student's height, theoretically preventing a shorty's view of the blackboard from being blocked. This unfortunately places me in the third row, amongst mostly girls. My big growing year is coming up; I'll get my revenge then.

I plunk down my briefcase and my lunchbox and slide into the seat. The class began fifteen minutes ago, and will resume now that I'm settled in.

There are notes on the blackboard written in almost perfect script. If I had written them, one would have needed the Rosetta Stone to interpret the writing. Left-handedness does not lend itself to intelligible writing, especially if your teachers try to 'convert' you. The very term, "left," translates in French to *gauche*, giving southpaws a distinct disadvantage. My right-handed fellow students were *adroit*, which also means skillful. This could also explain my performance at any sport requiring the use of the hands. I'm not the guy the captain picks first for his team, unless the captain is betting on the other team.

Since we are so close to the end of the term, the class seems relaxed. Some of us (not me) regret that there will be no school for over two months.

Mrs. Lee is reviewing what the class has learned in the past year. I seem to be up to date on geography, history, English and science, but it feels as though I'm years behind on mathematics. My attitude is why learn something you'll never use in later life? I can find no possible reason for understanding square roots—let alone geometry. And algebra? What were those Arabs thinking when they thought that up?

So I don't do well on the math quizzes, but show strong aptitude in the American history review. Reading history books at home has given me a distinct advantage, and I did learn some things that were not being taught in the school system. Maybe the Board of Ed didn't think young minds could handle some of the ways we treated America's indigenous populations. I guess we showed them Injuns…

I offer my opinion on that subject, and the mistreatment of Negroes. Several young toughs, in the rear of the room, immediately boo me. And since they are in the last row, I'm sure I'm a runt compared to them.

I choose the coward's way out and quit my ranting on the subject. Leroy, the only other boy in my row, has very dark skin and kinky hair. He looks at me, seeming to show respect for my point of view. It's entirely possible that those large morons have been disrespecting Leroy throughout the term. I say this because I have seen some white kids behaving quite nastily to colored boys in my last school. But at PS 25, the racial populations were pretty evenly divided, not like here, where you hardly see a colored kid.

I abhor prejudice. I hear it from my mother all the time. She still refers to them as *Shvartzes*. The term means "black" in *Yiddish* and German, but it is clearly used as a racial epithet. This does not make much sense to me, as a person of the Jewish faith, knowing what prejudice my own people have suffered throughout history. Ironically, most of the Jews I know seem not to show respect for dark folks. My Dad is different. He never uses insulting language to describe a race of people.

We're on to the English quiz. Aunt Chalya's language lessons have paid off, as I seem to have little trouble with parts of speech, punctuation and pronunciation. I display an air of self-confidence when asked to analyze sentence structure. Mrs. Lee seems impressed, but I'm hearing catcalls from the back row. The teacher is not happy with this outburst and threatens to take action. This is in the form of having to stay after school—something that is not very popular with the gibbons in the rear of the class.

Next term I'll be in the 7th grade. That means departmental—in other words, we won't stay in the same classroom for the entire day, but take different classes in different rooms. Why am I thinking about the next school session, when summer's just around the corner, when I won't have to even think about school? I won't have to worry that forgetting to zip my fly will make me a laughing stock, or that a bunch of roughhousers might want to rearrange my skeletal structure.

The noon bell finally rings. "Enjoy your lunch, children, and make sure you've returned to your seats by one," instructs Mrs. Lee.

Practically everyone, including the teacher makes a mad dash for the two doors. I grab my lunch box, expecting to head over to where I am told the cafeteria is located. As I approach the rear door to exit the classroom, I notice an obstruction. Its name is Billy. He is accompanied by two of his equally behemoth fellow thugs.

"Where ya goin', Hank?" says the freckle-faced redhead, whose girth fully blocks my exit. The emphasis is on my name in mock fashion.

"Yeah, Hank, where ya goin'?" the other two cretins chime in.

"Oh, I don't know," I reply. "But it's lunch hour, so I think you can figure it out." I say, still failing to realize that sarcasm might not be in my best interest. The words "don't do it," coming from that hidden voice won't do the trick.

"Whatcha got in the lunch box, Hank?"

"Don't' know," I say. "My mom packs my lunch, and it's always a surprise."

"Well, let's see it. Maybe we'd like to share it," comes from one of the others.

I look around the room observing that the four of us are the only ones remaining. It's unlike me to hesitate after hearing a bell ring. In my old school it was a stimulus response mechanism: Bell ring—fly out door.

My nervousness is now quite visible. "P..please l..let me p..pass." I stutter as beads of sweat begin to mount on my forehead.

"Scared, Hank?" Billy inquires as he pushes a bony finger into my chest.

"Just leave me alone. I'm not looking for any trouble."

"You may not be looking for it, but I think it found you," a Joe Palooka look-alike informs me.

"What did I do?"

"We don't like smart-asses, and we sure don't like guys who love niggers."

So that's it. I managed to wind up in a classroom with a bunch of racist goons. I'm beginning to think that the next few moments will not be my most pleasant. Then I look up to discover that my assailants have disappeared.

"You're still here, Hank," says the welcome voice of Mrs. Lee. "You'd better get going so that you'll be here in time to resume class."

The goon squad had obviously spotted her coming in the front door and quickly made tracks.

I proceed to the lunchroom, wondering just what three o'clock surprises await me.

Chapter 9 • Lights Out in Little Italy

"We got into a street fight. And the street won."

-Unknown

June arrives, and with it the freedom that comes with summer vacation. I cannot hide my glee over this annual occurrence. I'm actually caught howling with delight at the ringing of the three o'clock bell, indicating last class, until that most unwelcome of all holidays, Labor Day. I am not generally one to express myself so vocally, and am usually turned off by outbursts of celebratory screaming. But the end of the school year transforms me from my normal introverted self into obnoxious cheerleader.

"But I will miss homework," I think to myself, "yeah, right, and also Mrs. Morelli," thinking of that hateful math teacher.

I'm now free to think about summer pleasures. Yes, I will have to work more hours at the drugstore, but anything is better than that prison known as high school. I walk home in a daze, lost in thought about the lazy, crazy, hazy days to come. How many baseball games will I attend this season? That Sharon is a real sweet piece of ass. Not that I actually know what that means. I keep hearing the older guys talking about it, though. Maybe I'll find out this summer?

Chico Rodriguez zips around the neighborhood on the *El Pimpo Brougham* of bicycles. It is a 1941 Schwinn *Challenger*, in mint condition, equipped with every doodad imaginable. Those privileged enough to get a close up view of this classic two-wheeler, which Chico calls *La Machine*, can appreciate the loving care that keeps Chico's bike immaculate.

On the rear chrome fender is a license plate that reads *MAMACITA*, Spanish slang for "babe." Because this tall, slender Latino, who could be any age ranging from sixteen to thirty, is never seen without La Machine between his legs, the bike is likely a substitute for female companionship.

Two flags rise from flexible stalks on the Schwinn's tail: the Jolly Roger, and the red, white and blue flag of Puerto Rico. Each color on this national flag has its own meaning, and Chico is always proud to explain.

Chico doesn't go to school, he doesn't work, and it is doubtful that a rich father supports him. So it is a mystery how he is kept in streamers, headlights, horns and fur saddles.

On this warm June Saturday, Chico leans on a wall at the drugstore that is my part-time place of employment, sipping something from a cardboard container. He is resplendent in his white puffy shirt, tight jeans and footwear referred to as Stomping Boots. A menacing nail-studded garrison belt adorns his waist, that measures no greater than twenty-eight inches. A red bandana completes the look. Always friendly to the younger neighborhood boys, he constantly assures them that as long as Chico is near, they have nothing to fear in the neighborhood.

I arrive at Cohen's Pharmacy to take up my duties as delivery and all-around errand boy. I have a few minutes before my start time and approach Chico.

"Hey, man, how are you doin?" I ask my Latino friend.

I normally don't drop my 'g's, but I do so in deference to Chico, who always does.

"Never better, never better," is the reply. "Say, didn't you mention you were headin' down to Chinatown to score fireworks next coupla days?"

"Yeah, yeah. Me and my friends are going down there tomorrow. Fourth of July is almost here," I say, my English degrading with every sentence spoken to this unlikely associate.

"And Puerto Rico Day is not far behind on the 25th. So, we got to get ourselves those two-inchers, some cherry bombs, maybe a few T1's."

"Want to come with us?" I ask, appreciating the extra level of safety that would be guaranteed by Chico's presence.

Chico accepts my invitation and a meeting time is agreed upon.

Next day arrives and my two buddies Gopher and Arnie meet me at the subway station, in the hope that Chico will join us. After waiting in vain more than a half hour (six months in teen time), we finally head down the steps, sneak under the turnstile, and board a train bound for Manhattan. It is not rush hour, and the train is practically deserted.

"I guess Chico's schedule is too overloaded for him to join us," I remark, raising my voice so that I can be heard above the din and clatter of the moving train.

"Probably ran into one of his bimbos and decided he would prefer her company to ours," Gopher retorts.

"Or maybe those new flashing lights came in, and Chico has to get 'em on his bike," Arnie offers.

"Well, we really don't need him. I mean, it'd be nice to have him with us. No one would mess with us if we had Chico," I suggest. "We just have to look tough, and we'll be fine.

"Definitely," reply both in unison, but nobody looks convinced, or very tough for that matter.

With words coming over the PA, vaguely sounding like "Canal Street," we exit the train and head out to the street. On the way towards the subway exit, we walk along a corridor that has a natural echo. This is an automatic signal for a group of teenagers to burst into doo-wop. It would be unnatural not to do so. With me in the lead, we break into our version of *In the Still of the Night,* attracting many stares from onlookers, none of which show much appreciation.

We emerge onto the corner of Canal and Broadway, looking as tough as three Jewish fifteen-year-olds can, and immediately scan for purveyors of pyrotechnics.

Within minutes of our arrival, two toughs, close to our age, approach us, nearly consumed cigarette butts protruding from their lips. It's almost as if our arrival had been broadcast on WINS1010, the local news station, as well as our mission to purchase fireworks.

"Hey, how you doin?" asks the shorter of the two strangers. "Youze lookin' to buy fiya crackuhs?"

"Yes we ahh," I answer, in an equally tough sounding reply.

Arnie and Jerome nod in agreement.

"Well, youze came to the right place. I assume you got cash?"

"Yeah," I say. "We got dough," acknowledging that we had definitely come prepared for a purchase.

Arnie is wearing a *mezuzah* around his neck, in contrast to the heavy crosses displayed by our hosts.

"You Jewish?" asks the shorter boy.

Gopher, following the "act tough" guidelines laid down by me, replies, "Hey. Got a problem with that?

"No, no," assures the short kid. "Just aksin."

"All right, then," Gopher replies with the satisfaction of knowing that he is the victor in this brief verbal encounter.

Our "gang" is invited to follow the two young hoods in the direction of Little Italy where it borders Chinatown.

When we're several blocks from busy Broadway and Canal, we notice that one of our hosts has disappeared.

The next time he's spotted, moments later, eleven others of ages ranging from twelve, up to late teens have joined him. None are smiling. It is at this moment that the boys from Brooklyn come to the realization that this will not be your ordinary firecracker run.

Within seconds, a melee ensues. Fists and boots fly; groins are kneed; religious epithets are hurled—and none of this coming from our side.

Three bedraggled kids, with battle scars, including blackened eyes, cut lips, and a multitude of bruises, stand on a packed train headed for Brooklyn. The subway car, in this early rush hour period, is packed with homeward-bound commuters, who stare and point at our disheveled faces and clothing. We have been relieved of our bounty, our dignity, and any shot at a festive Fourth.

Chapter 10 • Country Blues

"When you come to a fork in the road, take it."

-Yogi Berra

A pair of monstrous hands shake my shoulders quite vigorously. At first I think these tremors are part of a dream in which my prom date, Bunny Goldenberg, and I are about to smooch in the stairwell near the gym.

In the dream, Bunny, the girl that I had somehow worked up the nerve to ask to the prom, by some miracle accepted my invitation. She looks ravishing in her hoop prom dress with low-cut top. She is probably the sexiest thirteen-year-old that I am likely to see, let alone be seen with. With lips awkwardly puckered, I am about to clumsily place my arms around her, when those same monstrous hands wrench my shoulders from behind.

I turn my head to identify the source of this unwelcome interruption. It's none other than Lenny Amalfatano, Bunny's much older, actual boyfriend. I can identify with the wildebeest about to become lunch for the raging cheetah. Then, as I emerge from my dream state, I realize that the hands are not Lenny's, but those of my father, attempting to rouse me from sleep.

"Okay, okay, I'm getting up," I mutter through sleep-glued lips. And if not for this obscene intrusion, would be securely planted on the pouting, puckering mouth of the lovely Bunny Goldenberg.

"Are you sure?" asks Dad, who's been awake since four, and expects everyone else in the household to be similarly roused. "You don't look like you're getting up," he conjectures.

"What time is it?" I ask.

"Five thirty, and we are leaving in fifteen minutes."

With that he leaves my bedside to continue the impossible process of awakening the remainder of the household. With the exception of Lancelot, who needs no one to wake him, Dad runs into the same wall of opposition from the rest of the family.

"Good dog," says Dad. "I never have to beg you to wake up. You understand about traffic, and how you have to leave early to avoid it." Dad must have gotten this from the *Train Your Dog About Traffic Patterns* manual.

The dog looks up at him quizzically, wagging his tail enthusiastically. Lancelot, A.K.A. Sir Droolsalot, although he's not known for his intellect, his loyalty never comes into question. He faithfully stood guard over the Katz residence throughout the night, as was his practice for all of his twenty-one dog years. What fool would attempt to enter our abode with the mighty Sir Droolsalot on constant vigil? Only those fearless of drowning in saliva, or of being leg-humped into extinction, would have dared!

As I allow myself to doze back to sleep, I hear my mother's high-pitched reaction to being awakened in the dead of night—a real treat for the ears.

"What time is it, Sol? It's pitch black outside," she screams—only slightly exaggerating the level of darkness.

"It's five thirty, Edie. We have to leave in a few minutes."

"I'm not leaving at any five o'clock in the morning, Sol. Let me sleep."

"Edie, you agreed to leave early so we could beat the traffic."

"Who agreed? You agreed. What kind of traffic is there at three in the morning?"

Dad tries charming her, which has the effect of a fart in a sand storm. "You look beautiful, Edie. Even when you wake up cranky."

"I'm not up, Sol. Leave me alone."

"But Edie…"

"Don't 'but Edie' me, Sol."

"I love you, Edie."

"Leave me alone, Sol."

After several 'romantic' exchanges my doze is halted by the slam of the bathroom door, and a flow of mirthless verbiage streaming from behind it. "No point in getting up just yet," I reason. "She'll be in there for a while, and then the place will have to be fumigated before anyone else can go in."

Sydney, who still shares my room, sits up in bed with a zombie-like stare.

"What time is it?" she asks, directed at nobody in particular. This seems to be the question du jour.

Only Sir Droolsalot hasn't asked it, but even he might have if he were fluent in anything but 'barkese.'

"It's five thirty-five," I say. "Why, got a date? By the way, I'm next for the bathroom."

"But I gotta go very bad," she whines, continuously opening and closing her knees and bearing the grimace of a victim of the Salem Witch Trials.

"Tough," I offer, sympathetically.

"Let her go next," Edie yells from the bathroom, defying the odds that she can hear our conversation through a closed door twenty feet away.

In a mocking gesture my sister sticks out her tongue and somehow, no longer seems to be in pain.

"Thanks," I say.

"Your welcome, Belch," she replies, using the cute little name she invented for me.

Dad paces nervously. He is dressed, and, in fact, has already packed the car. He chomps loudly on a carrot. Pieces of egg appear on his chin.

"Getting out of bed?" he asks, launching chunks of yellow, white and orange colored debris into the air.

"Waiting for the bathroom, Dad," I answer. "And she's after me."

"Before you," Sydney corrects.

"After me," I re-correct.

Just then Edie appears at the doorway of our room. Standing in a night-gown Sol thinks is irresistibly sexy, she admonishes me, "Act like you are actually older than your sister."

With that, Sydney flies into the bathroom.

"Want something to eat, Henry?" my mother asks.

"No," I respond.

"No thank you," my father interposes.

"No, thank you." It is hard to think about intake when forces are at work guiding me in the opposite direction.

"Have something before we go," she commands.

"He's not hungry, Edie."

"I'm not hungry, Ma."

"Well, get dressed. Your sister will be out in a minute. I'll make you a little something."

"Ma, I don't want anything."

"Leave him alone, Edie. He doesn't want anything. Besides, there's plenty of food in the car."

"What, hard boiled eggs? By you that's breakfast?"

"There's bread. There's peanut butter…"

"Sol. They will have a little cereal before we go and *hoc mir nischt in kopf*," a *Yidishism* she has used many times before. "Besides, I'm putting up coffee. You want?"

"There's no time. We can get coffee at the Red Apple Rest."

"Sol. I'm not waiting five hours for coffee," again demonstrating her mastery of exaggeration.

She quickly disappears into the kitchen. The clanking of pans is soon heard as she fumbles her way through the crowded cabinet to come up with the percolator.

"Sydney, are you finished yet?" I shout, as the pressure on my bladder is overwhelming.

"Soon," she sings back through the closed door.

"Sydney, hurry up. Your brother has to go."

"I am hurrying. It doesn't want to come out."

"Come out, now, and you'll finish later," Dad suggests, strongly identifying with my position.

I stand in front of the bathroom door, holding myself in hopes that the dam doesn't rupture. The sound of splashing water, from behind the bathroom door, conjures up visions of Niagara Falls, and that is not helping.

"Open up, goddamn it," I shout.

"Don't talk to your sister that way, Henry," Mom chimes in.

"Ma, I'm gonna wet the floor if I don't get in there, right now."

"Sydney. Open the door, this instant," Mom screams.

The door opens and I rush towards the bowl. "What the hell were you doing in there for so long?" I demand to know, which is heard over the surge of Hank Katz Falls.

"Washing my dolly," she answers, matter-of-factly. "…and I see Hank's poopoo," she taunts, using that word as a substitute for penis.

"Well, get out, and you won't see it."

"Henry, close the door when you go to the toilet. Your sister doesn't need to see that," Mom lectures.

I bite my lip, resisting the temptation to respond. I hear the rhythmic beat of the perc, competing with the equivalent of the raging Amazon entering the bowl in front of me. Taking in the aroma of the strong beverage, I'm convinced that my mother learned to make coffee while on a cattle drive in the old West.

"Sol, I have coffee almost made. You want some?" Edie asks.

"*Mahzoltov*," he replies.

The murky brown liquid is slurped to avoid third degree burns to the lips and tongue. The sound is audible three rooms away.

"Good coffee, Edie," he manages, always finding a kind word to say to her.

"An expert on coffee, I married," she mutters. "You put so much sugar in there, how would you know?"

At last we are all ready to leave. Sol glances at the clock. "Six fifteen — who ha!" he exclaims. "We're gonna hit traffic. I wanted to leave early. You all agreed to leave early."

Lancelot wags his tail as we gather up our bags, barking excitedly.

"Yes," we are taking you, too," the animal is reassured.

He barks again, which I interpret as "Thanks, I was hoping you would."

We get to the street and slide into the aging Pontiac. Four doors slam, breaking the silence of our Brooklyn residential street on this early summer Saturday morning. Then, Sol's door opens, and he makes a mad dash back up the brownstone steps to the apartment.

"Now, where are you going, Sol? You rushed my *kishkes* and now you're not ready to leave?" She calls to him.

"Sorry," he yells back from the top of the steps. "Nature is calling again."

"Announce it," she shrieks. "On the next block, they don't know that you're going to the bathroom.

"I've never seen a man go to the toilet so much, God bless him," she mutters. "He went three times, already, this morning."

I question if having so active a digestive system qualifies a soul for a blessing from God. If that were true, Dad is probably in line for sainthood.

"Do you want to eat something, children?" she asks.

"Ma, we just ate," we reply in unison.

"You ate nothing. Sydney, you left over most of your cereal."

"It's okay, Ma—I finished it," I say.

"You I'm not worried about. You're a human Electrolux. I have bagels, bialys, and pumpernickel. Sydney, which do you want?"

"Ma, I'm not hungry, okay?" says Sydney.

"Have one piece of bread. Have a bagel."

"But, Ma…"

"Have half a bagel."

"Alright. A half a bagel," finally cracking under the intense pressure of the Edie Katz Nagging System.

Mom rummages through the bag she is sure contains the bread. After a vain search through the rest of the food bags, she confesses, "I don't think I have any bagels. How about a nice bialy?"

Before Sydney can answer, one is shoved into her mouth.

Dad returns to the drivers' seat and is promptly derided by his wife. She keeps it up for the next half hour as we attempt to leave the city.

We are headed upstate to look at summer rentals. The plan is to find a place, preferably near a lake, where Mom and two children can spend part of the summer and escape the heat. Dad would come up on weekends, and we can be one big happy family, again.

Despite the urgency of leaving early to avoid traffic, Dad hates paying tolls. He'll do anything to avoid them, including driving an hour out of the way. He knows he can make up for the cost of the extra gas by coasting in neutral down the many hills in the Catskill Region.

The first toll to avoid is the Battery Tunnel, a newly constructed East River crossing connecting Brooklyn with lower Manhattan. Travelers can save up to an hour, depending on traffic. The problem is the toll of thirty-five cents. The Brooklyn Bridge is free, as are the other interborough bridges.

Dad decides to save toll money and take the Williamsburg Bridge. Unfortunately, many other drivers on that early Saturday morning have the same idea. We become stranded for forty-five minutes, mid-span, for reasons that are not apparent. Mom, who forgets that the whole world is not Jewish, is incredulous that so many people could be out driving at seven a.m. on *Shabbas*.

"I told you we should leave early," Dad shouts to everyone in the car. So full of wrath is he that even Lancelot holds his head down in shame (and he was ready on time). "I said to be ready to leave by five forty-five and I have to beg everyone to get out of bed," he rages on.

"Dad, why didn't you take the tunnel? Isn't it much faster?" I ask.

With this new ammunition, Mom is now free to open up with both barrels.

"Is that true, Sol? You mean to tell me that we could have avoided this if you had taken the tunnel?"

"I didn't think we would…"

"You never think. Do me a favor, Sol, next time you want to leave at the crack of dawn, leave me out."

Dad sits behind the wheel, tapping nervously on it. He is silent, but for a quiet whistle. His eyes stare up at the roof of the car.

"I have to go," whines Sydney.

"You'll go soon," her mother responds.

"But I have to go, now, Mommy."

"You can't go right now," says Dad, agitatedly. He is not having a good day.

"I don't know if I can hold it in," she moans, locking her knees together with her hands.

"You'd better," I say.

"Keep quiet, Henry. Not your business," warns Dad.

"Why didn't she go before we left?" is my natural question.

"I didn't want to hold everyone up," says Sydney.

"But you'll be holding us up, anyway," I argue.

"Shhhh," hisses Dad, his color becoming a bright red.

"You'd better shut up, both of you," says Mom. "Your father has to drive and he shouldn't get excited."

"Do you smell that?" I ask.

"What?" Sydney asks, apparently the only passenger curious enough to inquire.

"Someone let one out," I say.

"Henry…."

"No, someone really did. Sydney, was that you?" I ask.

"No," she answers tentatively.

"Are you sure? You just said you had to go," I remind her.

"Maybe it's Sir Droolsalot," Sydney suggests.

But he can't be the culprit because he shows no guilt usually associated with the commission of this act.

We finally make it off the bridge. Dad reluctantly pulls over to find accommodations for Sydney. This will not be easy, as most of the businesses on Delancey Street are Jewish-owned, and don't operate on the Sabbath.

We spot an all-night bar on the corner of Allen. It's the only choice available with the improbable exception of squatting at the curb, which is suggested but promptly rejected by Sydney.

"Take her in, Sol."

"Why me. She's a girl. Her mother should take her."

"What's the matter with you? Are you *mishuga*? I'm not going in there, Sol. You want me to take your daughter into a bar where all the drunken Goyim hang out?" Her memory, that people other than Jews also occupy the planet, has returned.

"Okay, I'll take her," I volunteer. "Anything to get this show on the road."

"Mommy, Hank can't take me to the bathroom."

"Alright, alright," says her Mom, and then looking at nobody in particular she moans, "I'll take her. So, your wife and child get molested by a bunch of drunken bums. It's perfectly okay. Just sit there. Come on, Sydney, maybe we'll get away with just a few bruises and some minor groping."

Dad, after having been successfully guilt-tripped by a professional in the art, relents. He disappears into the bar, sobbing little girl in tow, after slamming the car door almost hard enough to loosen it from its hinges.

After what seems like the time it took to carve Mount Rushmore, Dad and his relieved daughter emerge from the Allen Street Bar and Grill, he with a flushed angry look, she with a pouty but much emptied-bladder countenance.

As they approach the car, Mom utters, "Just look at the way that man dresses. You'd think he has nothing to wear. A drawer full of clothes he hasn't even opened yet. He has shirts from his *Bar Mitzvah* that are still in packages."

"Sol," she cries, "Where did you get that outfit? Were they having spring cleaning at the Salvation Army?"

Her husband, exercising a rare moment of good judgment, attempts to ignore her, continuing to walk silently toward the car.

"That shirt looks terrible with those pants. Who taught you how to dress, Emmet Kelly?"

I wonder why those critiques from the family fashion expert were not expressed before we left our apartment, when they might have done some good? After depositing his daughter in the back seat, he opens his door and attempts to defend his fashion sense. "What's wrong with what I'm wearing, Edie? Besides, who's going to see me?"

"I'm going to see you. In fact, I already saw you. No wonder I get nauseous on these trips."

Unfortunately, Dad never mastered the art of verbal self defense. If he had, he could have mentioned that his wife's outfit was probably hand selected by Helen Keller.

Now that Sydney's bathroom requirements have been fulfilled, at least temporarily, we are again ready to resume our journey.

Dad knows all of the Hudson River tolls, and prides himself in his ability to minimize the cost of a trip. He will avoid the fifty-cent toll at the George Washington Bridge, and pay only a twenty-five-center at the Bear Mountain Bridge. These economies don't factor in the extra mileage incurred, especially if you have no idea where you're is going.

He chooses the Bear Mountain Bridge because he likes the name, he says. The name "Bear Mountain Bridge" is superior to "George Washington," who, come to think of it, had nothing to do with the building of it, anyway.

I dare not reveal that I am onto Dad's cost-saving technique out of fear that it will unleash a tirade from Mom, who has never claimed patience as one of her virtues.

Sydney keeps asking where the bears are.

"I think one just got into the trunk when we stopped for the toll," I volunteer.

"Mommy," cries Sydney. "Hank said that a bear is in the car and is going to eat us all up."

The crew in front jointly echoes, "Henry, stop scaring your sister."

It was amazing, the degree to which Sydney inherited the exaggeration gene from her mother.

The route is quite beautiful, far superior to the faster, more expensive Hudson River crossing, connecting Manhattan and Fort Lee, New Jersey.

We are on U.S. 6, heading west to Route 17, gateway to the *Hebrew Himalayas*.

As we ponder the breathtaking beauty of the surrounding scene, a little whimper comes from the floor of the car. I look down at poor Lancelot, who, if it were possible, would be showing a green complexion.

I notify the captain that we have a sick passenger on board. Dad reluctantly pulls over so the dog can get some air. Unfortunately, relief comes a little too late to prevent him from spilling his guts.

"Sol, what did you feed him this morning?" his wife not-so-gently inquires.

"I gave him some of what I was eating," he replies. "He kept begging me."

"Tell me you didn't give him peanut butter, Sol."

"And a little bit of egg salad."

"Sol, what is the matter with you? You don't feed a dog peanut butter and egg salad."

"That dog usually eats anything. I didn't think it would do him any harm."

Dad walks with Lancelot, disappearing momentarily behind the trees aligning the road.

"I'll bet I know what he's doing in there. He didn't go to the bathroom enough today," Mom observes.

"Ma, stop picking on him, already," I say, disgusted with her relentless verbal assault.

"You, mind your own business, and not a word out of you either, Sydney…

I see that stupid grin on your face."

It's been many hours since leaving Brooklyn, but feels more like several days. A combination of toll-avoidance road experimentation, a general propensity to get lost, the need to constantly stop for bladder maintenance on the part of Sydney, and Sir Droolsalot's unsuccessful quest to assuage nausea are the reasons.

Dad only wanted to "beat the traffic," which was now sort of moot, and to arrive at Lake Wanasink well before noon. The trip normally takes less than two hours, but was it mentioned that normality was not part of the Katz family equation?

We finally arrive at the Schleppstein Country Colony to learn there is only a single remaining bungalow available for partial summer rental. Mrs. Gertrude Schleppstein, who looks much too young to have a name like "Schleppstein," gives us a tour of the cabin. Her job is not made any easier, as Mom finds fault with practically every feature of it. Each time Sol praises the owner for things about it that please him, Mom chimes in with a negative rebuttal. She finally pulls him aside, and in a loud whisper explains why complimenting is not a good negotiating tactic when you want to pay the lowest price for something.

Dad gets the message and keeps silent for the remainder of the tour, which takes little time, as the house has just three rooms.

The question, asked in unison, "Where's the bathroom?" is answered when the proprietress' finger points toward a small structure outside, adorned with a half-moon carved below its eves.

Edie and Sol excuse themselves to have a private discussion, before agreeing to the rental. He has no problem with the accommodations, including the lack of bathroom privacy. Mom, on the other hand, doesn't share his enthusiasm, but is willing to compromise her high standards if the price is significantly reduced.

After a haggling session more contentious than the Battle of Hastings, they come to terms and hand Mrs. Schleppstein a deposit.

We will be making another trip up there again in two weeks, in a car loaded with clothing, pantry supplies and sporting equipment. The five of us sharing a bedroom, Sir Droolsalot included, will be ready to enjoy a whole month of summer fun. I just cannot wait.

Chapter 11 • Getting Off Easy

"I believe the only time the world beats a path to my door is when I'm in the bathroom."

-Unknown

Ah, the first day of spring; at least that's what the calendar says. But, as is typical for the Northeast, winter takes its sweet time leaving for wherever winter goes when it's finally ready to part company.

Dad can't wait to get out into the open air. He thinks, eats and breathes nature, resisting the indoors as much as is physically possible. This past winter was particularly dreadful, with snowfall at record levels.

Our Pontiac wagon is not garaged, and still shows the vestiges of the last blizzard, its tires resting on mounds of slush, evidence of snowball battles on its windows, and about four inches of soot-covered snow on the roof.

But plans to go to Belmont Lake State Park in Suffolk County were made weeks ago, and my father was going to picnic or bust. Mom thought "bust" was a far better option, and packed our lunches most reluctantly.

"Why that man would want to go out in the middle of winter for a picnic, I'll never understand," she opines, confusing, as usual, the 21st of March with the ides of winter. The thermometer outside our living room window reads a balmy fifty-five, not exactly Fairbanks.

This time it wouldn't be just the Katzes 'enjoying' the great outdoors. Mom invited the Cavanaughs to share this day with us. We have a station wagon, more than ample to handle four Katzes and an equal number of Cavanaughs.

Sylvia Cavanaugh and Edie are fellow salesclerks at the E.J. Korvette's department store in downtown Brooklyn. Mom sells millenary to women who still wear hats, while Sylvia works in China (not the country—the department). They spend their lunch hours exchanging stories about just how weird their husbands are. It's doubtful that Mike Cavanaugh could be any more eccentric than my Dad. But, after meeting him at a softball game last summer, I thought he might be competitive.

I was far more interested in their daughter, Charlotte, who was two years my senior, making the girls in my eighth grade class resemble toddlers. I met her last year, during softball season, and could not fail to notice certain of her endowments. It was the first time I became aware that breasts were what make females stand out. She had become the object of my onanistic activities—most of my female classmates didn't quite fill that bill. Despite Charlotte's knockout figure (she was endowed by her creator with certain inalienable unmentionables), her face would win no beauty contests.

So, I was more than just a little excited when I learned that Sydney would not be the only young female in our entourage. It also meant I would have to put up with Dickie, Charlotte's aptly named younger brother. Little Richard Cavanaugh was a miniature carbon copy of his Dad.

Dad spends almost two hours getting the car presentable for company. He enlists my support in gathering up the tons of crap that have managed to pile up on the seats and on the floor. Dad supplements his income by doing garden maintenance, along with some other odd jobs. I have been assigned the task of removing any remnants of manure fertilizer, which play an essential role in gardening. Most people don't wait for a family outing (with guests) to remove cow shit from their vehicle. No rush, I guess.

The Pontiac is ready after the last snow has been brushed away. I enter the apartment to let Mom know that we are ready to depart. She is not exactly thrilled to receive this message, seemingly in no hurry to make her way down to where the wagon is parked. Lancelot, on the other hand, is very eager, wagging his tail furiously, and barking excitedly.

"Wha d'ja make me for lunch, Ma?" I ask her as we descend the brownstone steps.

"*Dreck mit leber*," she answers, which translates to "shit with liver." It's her unique was of telling me that whatever it is, that's what it is. In other words, "You don't get to vote."

Being so familiar with Mom's cooking—and the fact that "nuclear holocaust" is a setting on her stove—I conclude that her answer may not be far off. I make a disgusted face, which she and Sydney don't fail to notice.

"Henry is making an ugly face," reports my sister.

"Stop making an ugly face," Mom says.

The car is loaded with a dog and four Katzes. Sydney and Sir Droolsalot share the rear compartment, soon to be joined by Dickie.

Sol pulls up to the Cavanaughs' average house, on their average block, in this average Brooklyn neighborhood. The only things not average are the Cavanaughs themselves.

Sol and Mike could compete in a Worst-Dressed Male contest. Edie and Sylvia could do the same in the distaff version. Charlotte, on the other hand, doesn't seem to be a part of this family. She wears jeans, so tight that I wonder how she managed to get into them, and would love to have been witness to that event. A light denim jacket barely covers an abbreviated red halter beneath it. I strain to catch a better glimpse.

Charlotte has grown about two inches taller since the last time I saw her, and those breasts seem even more voluminous than before. I begin to salivate, positive that it's not the thought of my mother's food that precipitates it.

Hellos are exchanged, including some from Droolsalot. Sylvia joins Sol and Edie in the front seat, while Charlotte hops in next to me in the second row. Her Dad sits alongside her, leaving nothing but my imagination between wholesome Charlotte and me. Dickie will have to ride in the back with the dog and Sydney—his intellectual equals.

There is an uncomfortable silence in the car since the Cavanaughs came aboard. Mom has never been in a confined space with goyim before, which may be contributing to her discomfort. Dad throws the stick shift into first, and the Pontiac begins to cruise toward the Belt Parkway—gateway to Long Island.

A familiar "Are we almost there?" is uttered by one passenger in the rear.

Not sure if it is Sydney or Dickie, either of whom would reflexively ask that question within two minutes of our departure, on a trip that should take about an hour with a normal person driving.

"We'll be there when we get there," Mom replies. "Henry, give your sister and Dickie a piece of bagel," the equivalent of 'stuff your mouths and shut up.'

Dickie is unfamiliar with this food. Apparently, Jewish appetizing is not on his parent's preferred food list. "What's this?" he asks me, examining it from all angles.

"It's a bagel," Sydney chimes in. "Haven't you ever seen a bagel before?" she asks incredulously. Her speech is muffled by the effect of a mouth stuffed with the impossibly chewy wheat substance.

Tiny teeth deal with the herculean task of chewing and digesting this product, which has helped, put Sam's Appetizing Emporium on our four-star grocer map. I am more than familiar with this store, some days working there after school, lugging twenty-two pound hernia-inducing potato sacks up and down steep cellar steps.

"So, Mike," Dad says, finally breaking the silence among the so-called adult occupants, "what do you do?"

"Thought you'd never ask," Mike replies. "Cavanaugh's my name, and insurance is my game."

"I'll bet he hasn't ever once used that line before," I quietly mutter.

Dad is now trapped in a conversation he most definitely hoped to avoid. "What kind of insurance do you sell?"

"All kinds: home, life, auto, flood."

"Have there been many floods in Brooklyn of late?" Dad inquires.

"Well, not too many, but why take the risk? As a matter of fact, I'm glad you asked, because this month, and this month only…"

"That's enough, Mike," interrupts Sylvia. "The Katzes don't need flood insurance."

"Yeah, but what about the time Daddy made the water from the toilet go all over the floor? Ewwww," Sydney is quick to remind us. The trip out to suburban Long Island is filled with precious moments like this.

I can't take my eyes off shapely Charlotte, but the conversation in the car does nothing to enhance my chances of exciting her.

After at least eight "are we there yet?" inquiries from the rear seat, our station wagon finally rolls into the Belmont Lake State Park lot.

Mom takes the liberty of assigning tasks to help get the picnic going. Sir Droolsalot is the only exception, compelled to sniff every spot previously 'visited' by other dogs, ensuring a pit stop in each of those places. My Dad carries a large basket filled with a variety of comestibles, including a large brick of Limburger cheese. During our ride, its aroma could not fail detection by the olfactory senses of all, including the youngest passenger, who commented, "Ewww, did someone let one out?"

I get to lug a carton of Coca Cola bottles that weigh me down; Charlotte carries some blankets; her dad, the food supplied by the Cavanaughs. Sylvia handles barbeque tools. Sydney is burdened by a large doll she got from our Aunt Chalya for her birthday, while Dickie deftly manages his yo-yo.

We pick one of the many vacant picnic tables at lakeside. It's so early in the season that there is virtually no competition.

Sol, in an uncontrollable need to relieve himself, decides to use the woods, instead of the lavatories, located a short distance away. This is to the chagrin of his wife, who knows why Sol makes for the trees, and mutters her dissatisfaction under her breath.

Mike attempts to sell insurance to a family of squirrels perched in a tree, just above. Actually, he has no real hope of making the sale, but is really just practicing. Trying to convince a squirrel to up its liability insurance is no easy task. He is looking forward to the hoard of ants that will inevitably join us to share our food, while availing themselves of "hill" coverage.

At this juncture, and with lunch unlikely to be ready for at least an hour,

I ask Charlotte if she would also like to venture into the woods, although not for my father's reason for doing so. She meets this suggestion with a smile I hadn't seen before seen on the face of a female. Why this interest in me, I wonder? Then I conclude that her face is far from beautiful, and she probably receives few dating offers. We tell my sister to let our folks know that we are going for a walk.

"Can I go, too?" she asks, which shouldn't have surprised me.

"Yes, if you're ready to stomp on the snakes that the woods are just full of," I say. My answer is enough to dissuade her from pursuing her request any further.

We tread over a pathway strewn with crunchy fallen leaves that managed to survive the long winter. She reaches for my hand, as we walk, squeezing it gently. I feel a sensation in a very different part of my body that results from her touch.

After about fifteen minutes we arrive upon a cluster of trees, and despite the early spring nudity of their branches, they offer enough cover to ensure our privacy.

I'm in a place I've not been before, and I'm not just talking about Suffolk County.

Charlotte, who is at least a head taller than me, looks down at my face, and moves closer. Her body's essence has some kind of hypnotic effect upon me. In hormone harmony, two sets of lips pucker with eager anticipation.

As she draws closer, my arousal is further exacerbated. I'm feeling as though I might puncture my jeans with a pointed object. She can't fail to notice and moves her body even closer. As she leans down to kiss me, I catch a glimpse of the magnificent fleshy jewels that are barely hidden by the red halter top. After the new-to-me experience of several wet smooches, Charlotte, her face blushed red, reaches down to my thighs as her fingers seek my rocky fella center of attention.

"Getting a little excited, there, Hank?" she asks.

"A llllittle," I nervously reply, feeling sensations only previously experienced under more solitary circumstances. As she strokes me in that forbidden place, covered by a layer of increasingly stretching denim, she slowly peels the halter down, exposing her full magnificence. Nipples—which I've never before witnessed on anyone but my skinny young sibling and my mother, prior to weaning—stand at attention.

Seconds later, if that long, boom!

She smiles and moans as she continues stroking my forbidden regions. "Even more excited than I thought," she exclaims.

Is this what is meant by the expression Jewish Lightning, I wonder.

I am feeling like I can defy gravity, as the sensations slowly and blissfully wear off.

When I've recovered sufficiently to return to what I knew would be a culinary delight, we make our way out of the woods to find the Katz-Cavanaughs. Both Charlotte and I suffer from navigational challenges and wind up having to double back to the lakeside bench after going over a mile out of the way.

"Where the hell have you been?" Mom inquires as we finally approach the table. "We've been waiting here for hours and hours, and your hamburgers are ice cold." Again, Edie doesn't need to practice the art of exaggeration.

I stand next to Charlotte, a cold burger in my hand, and all eyes focusing on the evidence of our sin glistening on my jeans.

Chapter 12 • My Ideal Girl

"There is no greater glory than love, nor any greater punishment than jealousy."

-Lope de Vega

It's early January. Graduation is only five months away, and girls are setting their sights on potential prom escorts. The rules for this elementary school prom are specific with regard to excluding outsiders—no exceptions.

This is to the chagrin of several of the most popular girls in the eighth grade, most of whom are dating much older and far more "sophisticated" high school boys. One is even rumored to be going out with a college freshman.

To the developmentally advanced female population, the reasons are obvious. Eighth grade boys are immature babies whose interests focus on sports, both spectator and participatory, and scatological humor.

A thirteen-year-old male, with raging hormones in full tilt, concentrates his lust on a much more available partner: his palm. That's a mate that never says "no," and doesn't need to be plied with gifts or hear the utterances of clumsily expressed compliments. A hand never whines, "You never take me anywhere." I am one fellow who spends a good deal of time with the *Lady Palmala*.

After recently discovering the distinct visual attributes of females, I'm sure I want to get to know them a lot better. But my shyness prevents me from doing so. I yearn for the courage to approach my classmate, the lovely Stella, who has partnered with me on some recent science projects. Whenever she comes close, I inhale the soft, sweet scent of her shampoo, and the dance of the pheromones ensues. I've found myself staring at her beautiful complexion, sharply contrasted against my own acne-pocked face, then hastily turn away to avoid getting caught gazing at this unobtainable object.

I berate myself for lacking the nerve to ask her to the prom. She'd never say 'yes' to me, I presume.

A few months earlier, I was "exposed" to the older Charlotte Cavanaugh. She taught me a game she called, "Don't Probe Me There," in which young and clumsy fingers were encouraged to find their way into forbidden folds, all the while pretending to be searching for medical abnormalities. I was barely mature enough to fully appreciate what was happening, but felt a rising in my private area for the second time, while in the company of someone other than Lady Palmala.

The schoolyard is a convenient after-the-bell hangout until dusk. Then, depending upon the season, Lou, the late-shift janitor, locks all school-yard gates. His dark blue uniform shirt remains permanently open, at least three buttons down, to reveal a virtual forest of chest hair. He's a follicle factory, who can produce four o'clock shadow at eight a.m. He's never without the smallest stump of a cigar, tightly clenched in his horribly discolored, remaining teeth.

Dusk arrives, and Lou drags his slovenly self into the yard to encourage hangers-out to leave the grounds, or risk being locked in. It never occurs to him that most of us can easily scale the fence, either to leave or to enter the schoolyard. "C'mon, boys", he shouts, "Supper's waitin'. Time yez all went home to your mudders."

That evening a few of us return to PS 161, climb the fifteen-foot chain link fence and drop down into the schoolyard. Most have cigarettes, pilfered from our folks. We gather around to smoke, tell sophomoric jokes, and discuss the Dodgers, despite their having left Brooklyn for the West Coast eight years earlier. That betrayal still dominates virtually every conversation.

Along with the usual bevy of young adolescents, Frankie Rizzo's older brother Vince, joins the group. Like the janitor, he sports a sandpaper face. The older Rizzo boy just came from the barbershop, and dons a pretty good Elvis pompadour and long sideburns. The back of his head features the newly-popular DA, or 'duck's ass' look. His jeans are tight enough to make knee-bending a virtual impossibility. They're adorned with a garrison belt that matches a pair of black engineer boots. An impossibly long Pall Mall dangles from his lips, bobbing up and down as he talks. He has a Brooklyn accent you could cut with a stiletto, which, by the way, he is rumored to be carrying in one of those boots.

When Vince talks, all those around him listen, exhibiting the respect that only one who has made it all the way to sixteen can earn. The fact that the Rizzo's father is the connected Freddie the Finger Rizzo, adds to this cachet. At least, that's the claim.

Vince is not here to discuss baseball, or listen to fart jokes. He wants to talk about Stella, the lovely young thing who works after school at her father's diner on the corner of Nostrand Avenue and Union Street. According to Vince, whose authority is unquestioned, Stella is a ripe peach pining to be plucked. Not that baseball has anything to do with it, but he boasts that he has made it to second base with her twice. In his expert opinion, she will be his by the time this weekend is over.

All ears are on Vince, as he describes in vivid detail his familiarity with the contents of the curvaceous sweater of Stella Papadakis.

I fidget nervously during Vince's monologue. Uncomfortable could not begin to describe my feelings, hearing Stella discussed in these terms. After all, she was not just my classmate, but also the love of my life—my ideal girl.

I'm shocked to learn that the object of my affections could be cavorting with the likes of Vince Rizzo.

As Vince continues the details of his exploits, my cheeks grow more feverish by the minute. I now face a moral dilemma: remain silent—allowing what I'm convinced is a dirty lie and character defamation to continue—or confront the older boy and risk dismemberment.

Finally, I can stand it no longer. I say, "Vince, I know Stella. She's not the kind of girl who would do such a thing…"

His ire provoked, he turns towards me with an icy stare that could maim. "You callin' me a liar?"

"I'm not saying that. It's just that I don't think Stella would do those things. Maybe you have her confused with someone else?"

"Look, you little prick," Vince roars, "I'm gonna wipe up the schoolyard with you. No one calls Vince Rizzo…"

Before Vince can finish his sentence, I take off for the nearest fence. Vince gives chase, but is no match for a guy who runs track, and is one of the fastest kids at 161. Up the fence go I, clearing it before Vince even arrives.

"I better not see your Jew face around here," Vince warns, "or you might not still have a face."

It's the next day, and I'm back in science class. Sitting at the next desk, as usual, is the lovely, but reputation-stained, Stella.

"Hello, Henry," she says, which is met with a muffled grunt.

"What's the matter, Henry? Have I done something to offend you?"

"No," comes my tentative reply.

"Well, did I or didn't I? You're usually so much friendlier to me."

"Something is bothering me," I confess.

She pleads with me to tell her what the problem is.

"People are saying bad things about you."

"What bad things, and which people?" she demands.

"One person, a guy."

"Which guy, and what did he say?"

"It was this older kid, Vince. He said that he felt you up."

"Vince Rizzo?" she asks, quizzically.

"Yeah, Vince Rizzo, so you know him?"

"Yes, he comes into the diner with his friends all the time. That filthy bastard! I can't believe he said that," a scowl now replaces her usual passive face.

"Why is it so hard to believe?" I ask.

"Well, the idea that Vince would discuss me in that way is ridiculous."

"How so?"

"Vince is not interested in girls," she definitively states.

"You mean he's a *faygala*?"

"If you mean 'fag,' then yes."

"How can you be so sure?" I ask.

"Vincent Rizzo comes in here after school, and always brings an entourage of effeminate friends with him. They all take dance at the *School of Performing Arts.*"

I'm impressed with Stella's communication skills, using two polysyllabic words in the same sentence. "Then why is he saying this crap?"

"Probably just his way of hiding the truth about himself, and trying to impress his brother. What he's saying is bullshit, and most of the older kids would find it impossible to believe. Still, that son-of-a-bitch will be very sorry he said that," she says, referring to her behemoth brother, George.

"George could easily make mince meat out of Rizzo and serve it at our diner with a side of stuffed grape leaves."

She puts her soft hand over mine, and squeezes. "You must care about me to have let this bother you they way it did."

"It bothered me alright," I confirm. "When I said something to Vince, after he bragged about what he did to you, he threatened to chop me up in small pieces. I had to run away, and now I worry that he'll see me on the street and mess me up."

"You were very courageous to speak out like that," she says. "He acts tough, but that's all it is—an act. And I'm quite sure he doesn't want it known that he prefers boys."

"I'll talk to him when he comes into the restaurant," she assures me. "I'll explain to him that his secret is safe with me, as long as he leaves you in peace, and never, EVER, repeats those remarks. I will remind him that my fiercely protective brother would really not appreciate his besmirching my reputation. ”

My eyes light up with the knowledge that I will probably survive my adolescence. I then turn to my Greek Goddess and, with voice cracking, bravely ask, "Will you go to the prom with me?"

Chapter 13 • Is That a Bomb in Your Pocket (or Are You Just Glad to See Me)?

"The one advantage of playing with fire, Lady Caroline, is that one never gets even singed. It is the people who don't know how to play with it who get burned up."

-Oscar Wilde, A Woman of No Importance

This is the big day—a chance to show my fellow high-schoolers that I know something about explosives.

Things haven't been going well academically. Actually, they've been going dreadfully. Fortunately, I've become expert at parental-signature-forgery, which I've successfully used to hide my scholastic performance from my folks. They were either too busy making a living in support of our family, or too oblivious to notice that they haven't seen any of my report cards in several years. Those teachers' "opinions" of how well or poorly I'd done were issued twice each term, and required parental signature as proof that they're aware of their child's progress, or lack thereof.

My American History teacher, Miss O'Casey, is a cure for insomnia. Her teaching method, namely requiring rote memorization, takes all the fun out of what should be an important and exciting subject. I think that, should I ever become a history teacher, I'd make it fun, incorporating the music, art and dress of the period to bring the subject to life. "Yeah, like I'm actually going to become a history, or any other kind of teacher," I think. "Why would I? I can't stand any of mine."

So, she gives me a 'D,' not failing, but close to it. In fact, a 'D' was once considered a failing grade. Dad would be awfully critical of a 'D'—history being one of his favorite subjects. Fortunately, Mr. Katz will never get to see this grade on his son's report card, or any others.

I do better in English, pulling a 'C,' mainly because of a paper I turned in, which Mrs. Kurtz really liked. When averaged with my abysmal test scores, it brings the grade up from the cellar. Maybe if I focus on the subject matter, instead of Mrs. Kurtz' shapely body, I will do a bit better. I fantasize what a tryst between a Katz and a Kurtz would be like. What can I say? Hormones vs. Hank: no contest.

Math skills are not among my scholastic achievements. I'm just plain uninterested in the subject, and still see no way it can benefit me later in life.

The School of Industrial Arts, as its name implies, is not an academic institution. Somehow I was accepted into it by demonstrating, on the entrance exam, some aptitude for drawing. But even there, I can't come close to other students who display genuine artistic talent.

It might be concluded that my educational achievements are nothing to write home about, as demonstrated by my report card avoidance technique.

I may not be particularly popular with teachers, but I have more than enough friends—or those posing as such—to see what trouble I might get into next.

Today is where my propensity for doing exactly that will be demonstrated. I have put together a fun little package for my followers and me to enjoy.

Actually, the package isn't so small that it won't be noticed, as it sits in the front pocket of my jeans. I'm pretty sure Mrs. Kurtz notices it, but possibly takes it for a sign of my lust for her. Actually, it's an aluminum foil packet containing a combination of chemicals that, under certain conditions, can ignite with a rather loud report.

I count down the minutes, waiting the millennia that it seems to take for my algebra class to end. Thank you, Arabs, for inventing this subject. I doodle all over my notebook, in contrast to what other students are doing, namely, actually taking notes.

RRRRRING....

The sound of the end-of-period bell wakes me out of my drowsy doodling state. It also tells me that something exciting is about to happen, or more accurately, that I will make happen.

I grab my belongings and pat my front left pocket to ensure that the packet is still securely in place. My heart beats wildly as I make my way toward the 51st Street station at Lexington Avenue—my retinue following close behind.

We gather on the platform of the southbound local. One pulled out a few minutes earlier, emptying the area of passengers, and giving me ample time to prepare my surprise. We stand approximately where the first car of the next arriving train is expected to stop. After glancing up the platform I spot no inquisitive eyes cast in my direction. There are no *stinking badges* to be seen.

Comforted by my confidence that my deed will remain unnoticed, and despite that annoying voice warning me of the unsoundness of this idea, I slip down from the platform, onto the tracks, place the packet onto the track, duct-tape it down and test it for stability. Satisfied that it is firmly in place, I pull myself back up onto the platform. Most of my followers stare in disbelief, their mouths agape.

Another local is expected in about seven minutes. This will provide enough time for us to break into do-wop, with the station providing the proper echo chamber. *Shake, Rattle and Roll* is appropriately selected, as we count the minutes.

The PA announces, in barely recognizable English, that due to an incident uptown, the train will be several minutes late. This adds to the tension.

After completing a fine rendition of the Bill Haley hit, we choose a Little Richard favorite, *Rip it Up*, also fitting the occasion. As we begin singing the "having some fun, tonight" portion of the song, the rumble of a train is heard as it enters from the tunnel, drowning out our medley. It moves at a snail's pace, down the rails to the south end of the station.

Tension rises as the massive mass-transit vehicle approaches the target. It comes to a halt with a familiar screech, the front of the car obscuring the spot where the foil packet rests.

No explosion.

Is the device a dud, or has the wheel stopped right before hitting the packet? The smart money would have left the area, and wait for the next train. But, no. I encourage my buddies to board, as long as we don't ride in the first car. As we stand in anticipation, waiting to depart, another announcement advises that we are being held here due to signal problems.

It's the beginning of rush hour and our car is pretty full, and getting fuller, as more passengers arrive, taking advantage of the delay. A man in striped overalls carrying a signal lamp moves toward us. Can it be that I was spotted placing down the packet, initiating an investigation? I emit a sigh of relief as the transit man passes us, disappearing into the lead car.

"Watch the doors", comes over the PA, but sounds more like "Otch the oars." The train jerks as it lurches forward. This is immediately followed by the sound of a huge explosion coming from beneath the first car, with a simultaneous flash of blue light.

We come to an immediate halt, as panicked passengers hastily exit, some pushing their way out of the car's windows. Moments later the area is filled with more men in striped overalls and police uniforms. The choking aroma of sulfur dioxide is heavy in the air.

There is apparently no visible damage to the mechanical giant. This may not be true for the motorman's eardrums. The package is not designed to cause destruction, but simply to create a bit of a stir, and judging from the buzz at 42nd Street—Grand Central, the next stop—stir it does.

It's Friday—my favorite day of the week, just as June is my favorite month. For at least the next two days, I luxuriate in the knowledge that I will not have to be anywhere near a school. I think "at least," because I might decide to extend my weekend by playing hooky, which would certainly not be my first time.

I arrive at my school expecting adulation from those who had witnessed the stirring event of the day before, and possibly from others who may have heard about it.

When I'm about to take my seat in homeroom class, Mr. Prior, the tall and lanky Dean of Boys, along with two gentlemen from *New York's Fin-*

est, enter the classroom. After a brief consultation with the teacher, she and Mr. Prior point fingers in my direction. I resist the temptation to remind them of the impoliteness of pointing, as the dean, and two large members of the *paunchy blue line* approach my desk. "Henry Katz?" Mr. Prior asks, his eyes staring icily at me.

"Here," I say, pretending to answer an attendance call.

"Mr. Katz, would you please come with us," says Prior. "There is something we need to discuss with you."

I rise to follow the three men as the room buzzes with the chatter of students, most of whom are snickering.

As we approach the dean's office, I'm overcome with a sudden need to relieve myself. My request for permission to go to the boys' room is denied, promptly and forcefully. The hand that had only rested on my shoulder, now grips it quite firmly.

Prior sits down behind his big oak desk, but an invitation to make myself comfortable is not forthcoming.

"Katz," says the dean, sternly. "I think you know why you are here."

I have a feeling it is not to commend me for an act of community service.

"No, not really," I answer, with all the innocence I can muster.

"These officers are here because of a complaint we received from someone who witnessed your commission of a reckless act of vandalism—one which could have had dire consequences."

"Mr. Prior, I have no idea what you are talking about. What act?" I inquire with an almost convincing look of surprise.

At this juncture, one of the officers chimes in. He opens his notebook, and reading from it, recites in a perfect New York Police accent," You were seen puttin' an explosive on a subway track."

I wonder who among my cadre could have turned me in. "Who said that? It's a lie. Me? I put an explosive on a track? Why would I do that? No, no, that was not I. That was definitely not I. I did not do that."

This is where familiarity with the expression "He doth protest too much" would have come in handy.

Since these cops and I have not been formally introduced, I label the first, Officer Big, and the other, Officer Huge. It's the latter, whose head almost touches the ceiling, who continues reading from his notebook, "On Thursday, November 5, at approximately four thirty-five p.m., at the transit stop on Lexington Avenue and 51st Street, a witness has testified that a youth fitting the description of one Henry Katz jumped down from the platform, and placed an unidentified object upon the track. According to this witness, a southbound Lexington Avenue local pulled into the station, stopping right before making contact with said object. When the train attempted to leave the station, the object that said perpetrator was witnessed placing on the track detonated, causing panic among the passengers."

"That's terrible. I hope nobody was hurt," I utter in full sympathy.

"There were no injuries, unless you consider the soiling of a motorman's underwear an injury," returns Officer Huge. "Besides, since you were there, you already know that."

"But it wasn't me, I already told you," I protest. "Maybe it was someone who only looks like me."

Officer Big comes closer, a pair of bright shiny cuffs dangling from his rather sizeable right hand. "Put your hands behind your back, Mr. Katz. You are under arrest for the willful attempt to destroy New York City property, and endangering the lives of subway passengers."

"But…."

Four massive hands escort me out of Dean Prior's office and into a waiting squad car.

Chapter 14 • Stolen Moments

"Laws are spider webs through which the big flies pass and the little ones get caught."

-Honore de Balzac

Charley is one of five pharmacists at Cohen's, a successful Drug Store on Eastern Parkway. He has taken a shine to me, often telling me off-color stories while mixing ingredients with a mortar and pestle. Today he tells me about tincture of *cantharides*, AKA Spanish Fly. I listen intently as he explains how the substance can be used as an aphrodisiac. He warns me, a lad of only fifteen, that the drug can also be dangerous, and how some historical figures attempted its use, resulting in dire consequences. I make a mental note that should I ever be tempted to use this chemical for illicit purposes, I should think twice, but at my age, it's difficult enough thinking even once.

While we're chatting, a new prescription is handed to Charley. Preparing it will require a powder located in the store's basement. I'm told it's precise location, and dart down the steps to retrieve it. After five minutes in a vain search, I hear Charley yelling from above, "We need that powder this year!"

I continue my search for several minutes longer and finally give up. Returning to the store level I moan, "Can't find it Charley. Are you sure it's in the place you said it is?"

"If it had hair on it, you'd find it," he tells me, a wicked smile appearing on his face. This becomes the standard joke around Cohen's. "Let's put

74

pubic hair on every jar in the basement so that Hank can find it."

I certainly prefer Charley to Robert, who is a dour man who never has anything pleasant to say, except when attractive females hand him a prescription to fill. He tries to impress them by speaking in an affected British accent. They groan when he tries to get too friendly. Robert towers over every other member of the Cohen's staff, and he is oddly shaped. He wears his intricately patterned pants way up high, where his belt nearly touches his protuberant male breasts. From the rear, seeing his flat derriere makes me feel like I'm staring at a wall.

It's now five o'clock—quitting time for me. I make my way out of the store and head down to the schoolyard. Several boys, who are hanging around eagerly awaiting my arrival, greet me. My popularity is easy to explain. I have something that they want—packs of condoms that I managed to slip under my cuffs and into my socks before exiting the store. I am the provider of a unique service come to be known as *Scumbags to Go*.

For Billy, it's a three-pack of *Trojan Enz*, for Ralphie it's a box of *Sheiks*.

I'm paid the grand sum of three dollars for this entire delivery. It would have been difficult for these boys to obtain this product through legal channels.

I'm also known as a source for cigarettes, also difficult for youngsters to purchase—and small bottles of perfume.

The likelihood that either Billy or Ralphie will actually use these sheaths is slim, but it makes them appear as though their sex lives are more than just fantasies, enhancing their schoolyard reputations.

An older boy, at least seventeen, judging by stubble on his face, approaches me.

"Hey, I hear you have perfume at bargain prices," he says.

I never saw this guy before, and I'm reluctant to answer. "Don't be shy," he says. "Your friend Gopher told me about you. I could use some *Chanel No. 5* for my girl. Do you think you can help me?"

"I'll see what I can do. Meet me here tomorrow night, same time. And bring five bucks," I say, having no idea what the item costs to buy in a store, but I figure I'm safe by offering it for a pittance. Little do I know that a small bottle sells for about twenty dollars.

"Three," he says.

"Four," I reply.

"Deal."

It's Friday afternoon—my favorite day of the week. As I leave the school I know I will be missing it terribly for the next two days. And if you believe that, I have some nice bottomland I can sell you in Prospect Park for very little money. Arriving at the store, I see Sam, the candy counter manager, eyeing me suspiciously. Other members of the staff seem to be averting their eyes.

Last night the store closed early to take inventory. I wonder if my lack of a warm welcome is predicated on those results. Brendan McNulty, the store manager, is conferencing with several staff members, including our other stock and delivery boy, James. I can see him shaking his head while McNulty looks at him with his arms folded.

I discover that there are no deliveries scheduled and then go about my business of straightening up the counters, including cosmetics. In the aisle behind the counter I search for the *Chanel*. Upon finding a bottle in its traditional white box with clean black lettering, I ease it to the floor, and gently drag it with my foot so that it is out of sight. A voice keeps telling me that this is not a good time for me to pilfer this perfume. I've heard this voice many times, and want to tell it to mind its own Goddamn business.

I leave the area to wait for a time when it will be less likely that I'll be observed carrying out my illicit task.

It's time to sweep the floor. I grab the wide brush broom and start with the main selling floor, ultimately reaching the cosmetic aisle. It is here that I use the broom to drag the box to the dustpan, and surreptitiously drop it into the waste bin along with the other trash.

As part of my duties, I haul all of the trash bins out to the alley and dump them into metal containers that will be emptied by a sanitation truck. I grin as I think about the name, "sanitation truck." Could there be a vehicle less sanitary?

I get word that there is a delivery ready, and I'm to take it to an address near Washington Avenue. I hop on the bike with the prescription in the basket. I make a side stop in the alley where I just placed the perfume.

As I'm tucking it into my sock, I'm shocked to see McNulty, staring me down with those cold grey eyes.

He grabs me by the collar, and drags me back into the store. It is through the back door, so there are no customers witnessing this humiliating moment.

In the next instant I'm in his tiny office with the door closed. Now there is only that McNulty stare that could burn through a cement wall—and silence.

Nature abhors a vacuum, so to me the absence of conversation becomes deadly. I try to come up with an excuse but McNulty, even if he were born yesterday, probably won't buy.

"This is not what it looks like," I say.

Nothing.

"I know this does not look good…"

Still nothing from McNulty. He is allowing me to hang myself, a gift I'm not fully appreciating.

"When I took out the trash, I thought I remembered seeing that box of perfume in the bin, but paid it no mind."

"Uh huh"

"When I got on the bike, it jarred my memory. So I thought I would go back and look for it. Sure enough, I was right. Someone must have thrown it away by mistake. I retrieved it, tucked it away with the idea that I'd bring it back after making my delivery."

McNulty sits there, without a word and continues to stare away. Finally, he lets go with both barrels.

"I'm so disappointed in you, Henry. We all thought you were a terrific kid: smart, funny, and most of all, honest.

"We've just taken inventory, and there are significant shortages in every department you have access to, cigarettes, rubbers, candy, cigars. And now we know why. I almost called the police on James, because I was convinced he was our culprit. Good thing I didn't, because the wrong boy would have gotten busted.

"Can you give me one good reason why I shouldn't call the cops and have you hauled away?"

Tears roll down my cheeks, as I'm pathetically unable to mount a defense.

I'm a lucky guy, because, for whatever reason, McNulty does not summon the police. Instead, he calls my mother. She isn't shocked at receiving this call. Maybe it's because of all of the tableware she has lifted from various restaurants, and perhaps thinks she may have been a bad role model. I suffer the minor punishment of not being allowed to watch *Hogan's Heroes* with my parents, when it comes on tomorrow night. She will now have to walk six additional blocks to obtain drugstore items, now that Cohen's is off limits.

I've also lost many potential customers for the once-thriving *Scumbags to Go*.

Chapter 15 • Bored of Education

"Education is an admirable thing, but it is well to remember from time to time that nothing that is worth knowing can be taught."

-Oscar Wilde

There's that damn alarm clock. Can it be any more irritating? Can it really be seven a.m.? I have much to look forward to today. There's an appointment with my grade advisor, Miss Stevens, over some outburst that I allegedly had with my history teacher. Next on the agenda is a chemistry exam (like I need an exam in *that* subject). A hygiene class held each Friday in place of gym follows this. It's where I learn important lessons such as, "Be true to your teeth, and they won't be false to you."

I'm really going to have to hurry to get dressed, grab a bite of breakfast, pack my lunch and walk the mile to my high school. Mom used to make getting out of the house much easier when she wasn't working and did what mothers are supposed to do. Oops. Almost forgot to get my sister out of bed, and fed—and get her to school.

I'm ready to leave. But where is the little brat? If I'm going to stop her from playing hooky I have to find her first. Lately she has become quite mischievous, (wonder where she gets that from?) hiding out in places she thinks I won't look.

"I wonder where Sydney is," I say in an elevated singsong voice. "If I don't find her soon, I'll just have to leave her here alone. No telling what would happen then. Especially with those ghosts that have been reported in the neighborhood—the ones who eat little girls for breakfast."

She's not buying, so I will have to waste additional time searching all the usual places: not under the bed; not hiding in Dad's closet behind the brand new clothes he never wears. After exhausting all popular hiding places, I remember that there is one where I haven't looked.

I approach the bathroom carrying three days of soiled underwear that were strewn around my bedroom floor.

"Well, I can't find her," I say, loud enough to be heard in the Bronx, "and I'm already late. Let me throw my filthy shorts into the hamper and be on my way."

I lift the lid, detecting strands of her blondish hair protruding through the dirty linen.

"Okay, here it goes. Poor Mommy will have to wash these, if she can just get past the smell."

"Stop," she giggles. "I'm coming out."

"Did I just hear a voice?" I ask. "No, I must be mistaken."

I stuff my laundry into the wicker container and push it down. It's greeted by muffled grunts, followed by pleas for help.

"I said I was coming out," she screams, the giggles replaced by a whine.

"I see you're already dressed," I observe, "in an outfit heavily influenced by Dad's fashion sense."

"Actually, mommy picked it out," she says.

"I'm shocked," I reply.

We grab her lunchbox, which was packed by Dad, at the crack of dawn, before he left to work his first job of the day. Judging by the odor emanating from the box, Dad has not heeded her request of "NO LIMBURGER CHEESE."

After dropping her off, despite the voice in my head advising me to the contrary, I have a change of plans.

In my briefcase is the latest work from the British historical fiction writer Jean Plaidy, who writes under several pseudonyms. This one is an account of one of Henry VIII's numerous wives, and her effect on British history before meeting her demise by the axe man. This will give me something to read on the subway, which I will do, yet again, avoiding another boring school day.

Heading toward the station, only a short hop from Sydney's school, I pass several of my schoolmates walking in the opposite direction—i.e. towards school. They look at me quizzically, as if to say, "School's this way." I pay them no mind and continue toward the corner.

I stand on the crowded rush-hour platform. The waiting passengers are mostly adults heading into work. The rest: lovely young things wearing Catholic School uniforms. You would think their somewhat less immodestly dressed, nun teachers would frown upon those short plaid skirts. Glad to know that their Supreme Being is bringing the benefits of enlightenment.

Don't get me wrong. I am not singling out the Church. All parochial schools spread nonsense. There appears to be many alleged Supreme Beings, and many of the faithful fight to the death, in attempts to prove that theirs is the only true one. And as we Jews would say, "There's the right way, the wrong way and the *Yahweh*." At least this Jew does.

Waiting for the #3, I have a chance to observe other things besides shapely legs. A man opens a candy bar and tosses the wrapper onto the tracks. I want to toss him onto the tracks, but sanity gets the best of me. I try giving him a dirty look, but his head is buried in the *Daily News*. As my mother would say, "The stupid *Goyim* read the News, but we educated Jews read the *New York Post*." I equate, from that maternal wisdom and some of my own, that not only do the *Goyim* read trashy papers, but they also enjoy littering the subway tracks. Isn't knowledge glorious?

The train pulls in. There's a mad attempt to stuff over a hundred people into a subway car with the standing-room capacity of eighty. Needless to say, not everyone squeezes in before the doors make several attempts at closing. They finally do, but not before a lady's handbag becomes suspended, by its straps, between the two closed doors. A very unhappy woman can be seen pounding on the outside of the door in a vain attempt to alert the conductor inside the car.

We lurch forward, causing many passengers to fall against one another. I am lucky enough to come chest to chest with a student of Jesus. Needless to say, she is more embarrassed than I, but I have committed the sin of lust. I'll have to confess that to my Rabbi, first chance I get. Note to self: Make confessional appointment with Rabbi.

Many hands grope and thrash, and the handbag can no longer be seen hanging. The owner might be pleasantly surprised later by a phone call from a Good Samaritan who recovered her property, but more likely it is now the prize of a successful groper.

I have yet to decide which subway line to travel today. I've been on nearly all of them and have seen the far-away terminuses of each, including Van Cortlandt Park in the upper Bronx.

Most of those going to work exit this conveyance by the time it reaches 42nd Street, Times Square. With the thinned-out car, access to the subway map is now possible. I view it to determine how to get to a line I've seldom traveled. With a series of free transfers, I could be on the 'A' line, and make it practically to the end of Queens. Far Rockaway sounds as though it would be nice this season of the year. That destination will give me an opportunity to catch up on Anne Boleyn. There are quite a few possibilities in connecting with the A—all of which take time. No matter, that's something I've got plenty of.

I step into a nearly empty eastbound express bearing the 'A' symbol. Each subway car is a self-contained locomotive. I find the empty cab where the motorman would sit had this been the lead car. The privacy of this seating choice allows me to read my book and chomp down on my sandwich without disturbance.

We are now out in the open, on the elevated section of the 'A' line. I've wolfed down my lunch despite the early hour, and have read a few chapters of my book. When it came to wives, Henry really didn't fool around. Okay, maybe he did a little. If he anyway resembled his portraiture, he didn't get those ladies to lose their heads purely on his looks.

The clickety-clack and slow movement mesmerize me into a sleepy state. Despite the excitement of Tudor turmoil, I doze off.

My nap is disturbed by the presence of a uniform leaning over my private reading parlor. He shakes me by the shoulder and I'm now fully awake.

"Sonny," shouts the cop. "Mind telling me what you're doing on this train at this hour of the day?"

My watch tells me it's eleven a.m., and the sun glaring through the window confirms it. It takes a moment for me to regain my composure, but not enough time to think of a really good answer.

"Oh, no," I reply. "I must have dozed off and missed my stop."

"And just what school would that be?"

"Uh, the *School of Industrial Arts*?" It sounds more like a question than an answer.

"Wouldn't that be in Manhattan?" he queries.

"Yes it would, officer. You sure do know your educational institutions."

"Then how do you wind up on this train, which comes nowhere close to that destination?"

"Funny you should mention that. I have a great deal of trouble with these damn subways. I'm always getting on the wrong one. "

"You got some ID, like maybe a transportation card?"

"I do, but in my rush to leave the house, I left it at home. I had to pay full fare because of that stupid mistake."

I don't greet the words, "Please come with me," with much appreciation. I'm led off the train at the line's terminus. Large signs appear with the words, Welcome to Far Rockaway. Somehow, I don't quite feel welcome.

The patrolman escorts me a block and a half to *Far Rockaway High*—if you can call 'escorting' being held firmly by the shoulder. He parades me into the office of the Dean of Boys. After a dressing down by Dean Moran, who resembles the offspring of a marriage between King Kong and some unidentifiable creature, I'm issued what is affectionately known as a JD card. I'm told that I must carry it at all times, as it identifies me as the juvenile delinquent I am. I'll be sure to keep it right next to my transportation card.

Chapter 16 • Great Balls of Fire

"Give a man a match, and he'll be warm for a minute, but set him on fire, and he'll be warm for the rest of his life.

-Unknown

Axel Fischer lives in a fourth-floor walk-up in the same building as the *Wearin' o' the Green Tavern*. His untidy bedroom is above its entrance. The three stories separating them is hardly enough to keep the joint's high noise level from wafting up to his window, filling his parents' apartment with the ceaseless cacophony of Celtic music, clanking barware, and the howling of its less-than-sober trade.

Wearin' o' the Green is a typical working-class bar, found in many Brooklyn neighborhoods. Inside, very little effort has been expended on housekeeping, evidenced by the myriad of stains adorning the floors and walls, and the missed targets of brass spittoons badly in need of polish. Ashtrays are never emptied, their ever growing mountains of butts overflow onto the ancient mahogany bar in endless cascades.

Tall and gawky, Axel can pass for the minimum drinking age without any problem. He is, in fact, two years shy of the age of majority. The rest of us are almost sixteen, and barely look even that.

"Here," says Axel. "Take my brother's draft card," handing it to me. "Now they can't refuse to serve you."

Axel has managed to acquire the card on a temporary basis from his teetotaler brother's dresser drawer. We haven't walked five feet into the smoky chamber when the proprietor, Red Herlihy, confronts us from behind the bar. His ponderous belly, covered by a well-stained apron, and his behemoth hands do not go unnoticed.

"Hey, young fella. Now what would you be wantin' in my bar?" the rusty haired and red-faced Herlihy inquires with a cherubic smile and the thickest Irish accent one would be likely to hear outside of Dublin.

"A b.b.beer," I answer in an almost audible voice.

"Speak up, young fella. I kin hardly hear ya."

"A beer," I repeat, with the cracking voice of adolescence, in a miserably failed attempt to lower my vocal timbre.

I catch sight of my flushed face in the long mirror behind the bar, barely recognizing my pockmarked, forlorn countenance.

"Well I still can't hear ya. You know we don't serve Pablum, here," speaks the jovial Red—to the enjoyment of his patrons who, without exception, bellow with laughter.

Drinkers in various stages of inebriation howl, but what is most embarrassing is the reaction of the female patrons, who seem to be thoroughly enjoying themselves at my expense.

"And even if we did," Red continues, "I think we're fresh out of bibs."

This produces a tidal wave of cheers and merriment based on humor I have difficulty appreciating. Like an injured dog, with tail between my legs and head lowered, I turn and slink out of the old gin mill, vowing never to return.

I emerge onto the street with my eye sockets filled with salty tears, and I imagine folks on the Upper West Side of Manhattan clearly hearing my sobs. I see Axel's long shadow on the sidewalk, easily dwarfing my own.

"You shudda held your ground," Axel says. "You couldda flashed Aaron's draft card. That's why I gave it to you."

"Aaron is twenty-freaken-two, and I look twelve, so screw you and your brother's draft card," I manage, between sobs.

Axel's grimace turns into a weak smile as he utters the words, "I'll have the yellow phosphorus tomorrow." This is his attempt at cheering up his clearly depressed friend.

My band of pyrotechnic wizard wannabees has been eagerly awaiting this announcement. Axel is the only one in the group who can pass for the age requirement to legally purchase this product from the Chen Chemical Company.

"Okay," I grunt, as the good news fails to quell my self-pity-induced malaise.

I imagine what I might do to the big red slob behind the bar as revenge for what has just been perpetrated upon me. Could yellow phosphorus play some kind of role? I ponder this as I return home to sulk, forgetting that this is my mother's night to host her weekly *Mah Jong* game.

When I turn the key into the second floor entrance, atop the long set of brownstone steps, I'm greeted by the sounds of seemingly dozens of high-pitched female voices. The clack of shuffling the little ivory tiles fills the vestibule, muffling the shrill female chatter. I enter the floor-through apartment, about to pass the room in which four women of middle age sit around a bridge table.

Something about this activity has always fascinated me. I stand transfixed in the doorway and I'm promptly ignored by all of them—my mother included. Edie stands, pouring a cup of coffee from a large urn next to the old Spinet piano. Mom's guests are seemingly deep in conversation.

Strangely, every woman speaks independently, as if no others are even present. One of them mentions her daughter's name in conjunction with an impending marriage to a dentist—a Jewish mother's equivalent of winning the Nobel Prize. Another player bemoans her husband's kidney stone. The word "oy" is repeated several times by a woman who is unfortunate enough to be within listening range. A third *Mah Jonger* has just returned from Grossinger's in the Catskills, and raves about the food, not to mention the comedians, "who are filthy, by the way." The woman with the Nobel, a Sadie somebody, complains of the oppressive heat in the Katz apartment.

"What are you talking? Maybe you're having hot flashes," My mother sneers. Her tone is meant to discourage any rebuttal, as she drops three sugar cubes into her fine china cup. I need no reminder that it's necessary to mask the flavor of Edie's coffee with as much sugar as possible, although there may not be enough sweetener in the world to accomplish that herculean task. I'm well aware of the nightmare known as her coffee, having once made the unfortunate mistake of tasting it. Juan Valdez would not approve.

Her remark to Sadie is the first instance of actual dialog since my arrival. They continue their monologues, oblivious to one another. Players call out tiles, as they become exposed on the table.

"Four Bam," shouts Mom's old friend Jeanne Weinstein, who takes up almost two seats.

"Five crack," chirps another, followed by, "he had better pass that stone soon, or there is no living with that man."

 "West!"

I've watched this game played countless times and still haven't grasped its concept.

"*Mahjong*!"

The room buzzes with chatter, followed by the raking and shuffling of tiles. Edie sits down, replacing Jeanne, as if any one person could.

"I'm home," I sing out, which has the impact of a microbe landing on the cheek of an elephant's backside during a sandstorm.

"Nice to see all of you, too," I continue. "And Jeanne, nice to see all of you, as well."

Jeanne is too busy stuffing her face with the Ebinger's cake that I had earlier procured for my Mom, from the popular bakery just down the street. She either fails to notice my sarcasm or chooses to ignore it.

I walk into the bedroom I'm forced to share with my ten-year-old sister. She's already fallen asleep, amazingly having done so despite constant cackling from the next room.

It is becoming increasingly difficult to share a room with my young sibling, especially now that I am approaching manhood. There are certain unmentionable tasks more easily accomplished without the possibility of the little brat waking up and noticing my quilt rising and falling rapidly without apparent explanation.

Under the covers I slip into pajamas, laying my head down on the very flimsiest of pillows. "Screw brushing my teeth," I tell myself. I'm still recovering from the incident at *Wearin' o' the Green*, but close my eyes to the thoughts of yellow phosphorus.

A group of my buddies and I sit in the not-so-originally-named *Olympus Coffee Shop*, at a booth in the rear—the less visible to other patrons the better. On the table are four tall Coke glasses, long emptied of their original contents. My glass, having formerly held a chocolate Coke, brims with cigarette butts, straw wrappers, napkins, sugar and ketchup dumped in for absolutely no reason. The other glasses contain varieties of similar refuse.

Stella Papadakis, the owner's lovely daughter and my former prom date, visits our table every fifteen or so minutes to ask us if there is anything else we want.

"What do you have in mind?" I ask for the umpteenth time. These remarks never fail to produce a shy, slightly embarrassed smile on Stella's innocent face. I try to exercise extreme caution when making salacious remarks to young Stella. George, her ever-watchful twenty-year-old brother, with the physique of a mountain gorilla, but with a considerably poorer vocabulary, would not hesitate to use my small intestine as an inner tube.

We impatiently await the return of Axel, who is on his Canal Street mission to obtain phosphorus. Axel is well known at Chen's, having visited there multiple times, returning with such goodies as metallic sodium. That element has the potential to ignite without the aid of any kindling device.

Alex purchased, from Chen's, chemically pure potassium chlorate, powdered magnesium and potassium permanganate, which when combined can produce the most brilliant purple and white flares—and at this moment, yellow phosphorus! This will be our virgin experience with an element that glows in the dark, and is extremely volatile, even with the slightest heat elevation.

Hymie Wasserstein arrives at the booth and slides in next to me. His left forearm bears the evidence of a childhood partially spent in Treblinka. Although barely sixteen, he has a sandpaper face that should be shaved multiple times daily. He came to America with what was left of his family only two years ago, and struggles with English.

When asked his name, he almost always answers, "Hymie Vasserstein vid a doble-u."

"Is that Hymie Vasserstein?" I asked him the first time he introduced himself.

"No, "Hymie Vasserstein—that's Vasserstein vid a doble-u."

This was a guaranteed laugh for Hymie's easily entertained fellow teenagers, whenever Hymie was goaded into repeating his name.

Robert Broke, who it was predicted would become a lawyer by his seventeenth birthday, convinces Hymie that when the phosphorus arrives, he would be the best person to carry it. The rest of us remain silent during this masterful act of persuasion, because certainly none of us would dare to volunteer.

Stella comes to the table to inform us that her father would very much appreciate it if we could settle our check and exit his fine establishment. This is not an unreasonable request, seeing that we'd spent the last four hours shooting straw wrappers, igniting matchbooks, and playing table penny football in his coffee shop while spending a grand total of sixty cents.

Axel enters the diner just as we're about to leave. All eyes are on him as a manila envelope is spotted under his arm.

"Did you get it?" I ask, practically drooling.

"Get what?" he answers with a smirk. "Just kidding. Yeah, I got it."

We pay the check, leaving a whole quarter for Stella for yeoman's service. She is left with the revolting task of cleaning up mustard, relish and other condiments that managed to find their way onto seats, walls, floor, etc.

We follow Axel the two short blocks to his place and climb to the top floor. The memory of the *Wearin' o' the Green* incident returns to haunt me. It's impossible to avoid the tavern, as it practically guards the entrance to Axel Fischer's walkup.

After a long trudge up four sets of creaky stairs, we arrive at his door. The apartment is dark, indicating that neither his folks nor his brother are at home.

"Ma?" he calls out, just to make sure she is not asleep in the next room.

Of course, had she been, she would not be now. With no answer from his mother, he switches on a hall light and we walk into his bedroom. The luminescence of a street lamp floods the unkempt room.

Axel nervously opens the clasp on the envelope, containing a second envelope, and then a third made of thin translucent paper. He pulls down the window shade and an eerie glow is visible from the envelope. I imagine us all in tribal costumes, genuflecting.

He places the contents of the small packet into a square of aluminum foil, bending in the sides to secure the volatile substance.

"Who's gonna carry it?" he asks.

"Me," responds Hymie, proudly.

"Really?" questions Axel.

"He's the right man for the job," says Bob. "He's been through danger before."

"Vot danger?" asks Hymie, with a new look of doubt on his face.

"No danger, as long as you don't heat it," I reassure him, passing Bob a supercilious glance.

"Oh", Hymie replies, and then somewhat confidently inserts the foil packet into his front pants pocket, as we make our way down to the street below. Destination: the schoolyard.

We walk at a determined pace, eager to get to PS 161 and a schoolyard, which we hope will be empty. The plan is to open the packet of foil in the middle of the yard, watch it glow for several minutes and then see how far removed a lighted Zippo needs to be from the substance to cause ignition. As previously mentioned, we are easily entertained. We come within a half block of the schoolyard entrance, only to spot a police car occupied by two members of *New York's Finest*. We make a quick decision to keep walking past the school and approach it from an unguarded entrance.

Some unidentifiable words can be heard from the lips of Hymie, who appears more than a little distraught. His face breaks into a voluminous sweat as his hand tries to enter the tight jeans pocket where the foil is working its magic.

"Oy, I think my balls are on fire!" he screams.

We stare in utter shock at his pocket, noticing wisps of smoke escaping from it. Hymie's fingers clutch the end of the foil packet as it becomes engulfed in a luminous burst. He tries dropping it, but the partially molten foil sticks to his hand. Had the packet been extricated five seconds later, the continuance of the Wasserstein family line would be in serious doubt.

Hymie sits on the ground moaning, with a thumb swollen to the width of a silver dollar. The front doors of the squad car open simultaneously and two men in blue emerge. The cops approach us with as much speed as their overweight bodies can muster. We pull Hymie to his feet, and take off in different directions. The rotund members of the constabulary do not give serious chase.

I choose a circuitous route to my folk's apartment, finally arriving twenty minutes later, soaked in perspiration. My mother and father are sitting down getting ready to watch the *Smothers Brothers* on their ten-inch Admiral TV.

My mother greets me with, "Oh hello, Henry. Just look at you. Why are you all perspired? Look at how he's *shvitzing*, Sol."

The lame excuse I offer goes unchallenged, as continued discussion might result in their missing part of their favorite new show.

"You want to sit and watch with us? Tom and Dickie are coming on in a few minutes."

Somehow the idea of sitting with my parents, while my father snacks on a peanut butter and onion sandwich, is not my idea of a great time.

Empathizing with poor Hymie, and thinking that it should have been Red Herlihy whose family line was threatened, I answer, "Na, I think I'll just go and listen to my new Jerry Lee Lewis record."

Its unusual title would now have a whole new meaning.

Chapter 17 • Lottie's Luck

"How do you know when your girlfriend is putting on too much weight? She starts fitting into your wife's clothes."

-Unknown

Everyone in the Katz family was pissed at Herbie Ginsburg. Nobody ever thought that Aunt Lottie's marriage to this loser was a good idea, with the possible exception of Lottie herself—and even she had her doubts. She deserved much better, but unfortunately she didn't think so. Her low self-esteem dictated that she accept a proposal from practically any man who would extend one.

Herbie was a habitual smoker of cheap cigars, and his choice of attire left much to be desired, never wearing two articles of clothing that matched. His favorite ensemble, reserved for formal occasions, was a polka dotted shirt and striped tie with plaid slacks. Every now and then he wore two matching socks. By comparison, Herbie made my father look like a model on the cover of *Gentlemen's Quarterly*.

Herbie's proposal came at her life's lowest point. At the age of thirty-nine, she had been fired weeks earlier from her job as a legal secretary, when it was discovered that the books she was assigned to keep were not exactly in pristine order. Serious money went missing, and the trail led directly to Lottie. She was with the firm for seventeen years and had been trusted by both her boss, and the other senior partners.

With her dismissal came the loss of her pension and a stained reputation that would make it virtually impossible for her to work in that industry ever again—at least here in New York.

Without a salary, a denial in unemployment benefits due to her actions and no other means of support, she felt desperate.

Mom comforted her younger sister as much as was possible under the circumstances.

I remember walking into the kitchen to discover Lottie bawling away, my mother's arms wrapped around her and patting her on the back. "You'll get another job, Lott. *Dingle and Dingle* is not the only law firm in New York."

Only I knew the real reason, because Lottie told me right after it happened. She then swore to me to secrecy—and because of our closeness, I promised it would remain our secret.

Lottie fabricated a story of why her employment had ended. She told Edie that she quit because one of the partners was constantly pinching her ass, and she was sick of it. In truth, Lottie only fantasized about those tushy tweaks, so her complaint served the double purpose of fulfilling her dreams and providing a convenient excuse for her unemployment situation.

I'm not sure why she was willing to make me, an acne-pocked adolescent, her confidant. Maybe it was because of the secrets we told each other, beginning when I was about five. And with all she has done for me, I vowed not to betray her trust. I remind myself of all the times she took me into "the city" (we Brooklynites refer to Manhattan as "the city") to see the circus or a rodeo at Madison Square Garden. I recall my first trip to the top of New York's tallest building, the *Empire State*, accompanied by my aunt, who exposed me to majestic views I'd never before seen. My sole previous exposure to that edifice from that vantage point had been in the screening of King Kong.

As we stood on the building's famous Observation Deck, we speculated on what would happen to the head of passers-by, if a penny were dropped on it from such an altitude.

I flash back to a memory a few months earlier: It was of my aunt and me, sitting in the *Automat*, one of several *Horn and Hardart* restaurants in the midtown area. I had just returned from the vending wall, where food is kept in glass cages, awaiting a deposit of anywhere from fifteen to twenty-five cents to dispense the world's most delicious macaroni and cheese (according to my high standards), or their glorious baked bean casserole, along with a host of other treats.

"Herb proposed to me last night," Lottie said, as I was about to swallow a mouthful of macaroni. The news caused me to expel most of my mouth's contents all over the table. Of all the people that Lottie could possibly end up with—why him, I wondered, as I embarrassingly tried to wipe the detritus off the table top with my napkin.

"Are you alright," she asked, alarmingly, concerned that I might have been choking.

"I'm fine, fine," I assured her. "Just a little surprised, that's all."

"Yes, I know you are not exactly fond of Herb," she said, "but we have been seeing each other for some time, and I know he loves me." As she spoke, I could see the skin above her elbows twitching, a nervous affliction shared by the women in our family.

I began adding up all of the reasons why every member of our family detested Herbie. In fact, he was the only human, and I use the term generously, that my Dad had nasty things to say about. Sol never spoke badly of anyone else, so I was convinced that Herbie's besmirched reputation was well earned.

"But Aunt Lottie," I offered, "doesn't your boyfriend have a problem with, er, gambling?"

"He used to, but he swears to me that he's over that," she replied, but the look on her face suggested that she only half believed it.

"Does the money missing from your former company have anything to do with helping Herbie out?" I queried.

She dodged the question and suggested that in order to catch today's live performance of the Ed Sullivan Show, for which she had a pair of tickets, we had to move fast. Thus she was spared from any real assessment of what her new life might resemble—namely a disaster.

A year later, upon returning home from an adventure with my hoodlum pals, I found Lottie sobbing away uncontrollably at our kitchen table. Edie and Sol sat close by, attempting to console her, Lottie's tears flowing in close competition with Niagara Falls.

"That son-of-a-bitch," I heard my father say, cursing for the first time in my seventeen years as a member of this household. To my knowledge, my father never before uttered an expletive.

"I tried to warn you," said Edie.

But this was not a lecture Lottie most appreciated at this moment. She was well aware that hubbie Herbie had made off with savings she had in "their" account. It amounted to close to twenty thousand dollars; the result of her almost miserly lifestyle, save for treating me to an occasional lunch and sundry events around New York.

As a shipping clerk (as opposed to a shipping magnate), Herb never made any real money. This hadn't stopped him from continuing to piss away their (her) savings, either at the track, or on the phone with his bookie, Ralph Gonanzanno.

Ralph, not known for his patience, had demanded his money, which Herb claimed he lacked the funds to pay. Unbeknownst to Lottie, Herb had managed to siphon off some their money, then probably used it to "disappear." It was also possible that Ralph and his minions made that disappearance happen. All we knew was that Herb was nowhere to be found, nor were the 20 g's

All of this drama prevented Edie and Sol from realizing how soaked with perspiration my shirt was when I entered our apartment.

Me, and my fellows in crime, Raymond and Rich, were nearly nabbed by a man in blue while attempting to relieve a white Caddy of its hubcaps.

The only thing saving our asses was the fact that we were all members of the school track team. We could really move, while the flatfoot could barely drag his bovine torso. So in lieu of any attempt to chase us, he yelled "Stop…" after blowing his whistle several times.

Needless to say, his "suggestion" was ignored as we each made off in separate directions. This was the second time putting feet to ground saved me from the arms of the law.

Back to Lottie. I felt really bad for her. I tried to think of ways to get some justice for my beloved aunt. I perused the *New York Post*, daily, in hopes of learning something about my prick of an uncle. After a few weeks I spotted the following article towards the back of the paper:

Man's Body Found in Trash Bin Near Williamsburg Bridge

I wondered if it could have been Herbie (one could always hope), so I continued on. After a careful reading, it was becoming ever more possible that this was indeed the gambling Ginsburg. According to the description, the body fit the age, race and physique of my uncle. Finally, towards the very end of the article, "the man, with a broken cigar stuffed in his mouth, was probably on his way to a masquerade party, dressed in an odd outfit."

That sounds like Herb, dressed in clothing unlikely to be seen in a *Barney's* store window.

Chapter 18 • Diddler On the Roof

I know something even worse about my late Uncle Herbie. It's so terrible, I have vowed to keep it to myself, avoiding the risk of upsetting poor Aunt Lottie and making her even more miserable than she already is.

Our apartment is on the ground floor of a six-floor structure. Aunt Lottie also lives here, as did Uncle Herb—until his demise.

As members of the working-class poor, my parents don't own a set of those newfangled washers and dryers. Edie wants them badly; understandable, based on the volume of dirty laundry that this family of four can generate. Dad's gardening jobs make doing a wash load a herculean task. Every chance she gets, she attempts to make Sol feel guilty for his unrelenting miserly refusal to part with the money the family doesn't have.

"It's okay, Sol." She whines. "My needs are not important. So what if I work in that *farcockta* department store all day, come home; make dinner; clean the house, and then face a load of filthy, disgusting clothes sitting in the hamper?"

"But Edie, we don't have the money. I'm already working three jobs, and we still can't make ends meet," groans Dad.

Anyone listening to this conversation would not need to be peeling an onion for those tears to come pouring out.

For most families living here, a washer is a sudsy, corrugated metal board, and the dryer is a clothesline located atop the building's roof. I have brought laundry down from there many times. I lack the dexterity to hang the wet clothing, or I'm able to convince Mom that I failed "hanging" in school.

I ride the elevator to six, and head for the stairway to the roof, with empty laundry basket in hand. Opening the roof door, I can't fail to take in the beauty that is underwear of all sizes and shapes, billowing in the wind, like flags in a parade. There is one particular pair of undies that could have been the national flag of *Bigassia*. Several women in the building could have simultaneously fit into them.

I get near the spot where Lottie usually hangs her laundry, and it reminds me of the day, months ago, when I spotted, between windswept sheets, the figure of Herbie, whom I assumed was also there to perform laundry functions. There was no mistaking who the clown in the unique attire could be. Only he wasn't alone. Each time the wind increased in intensity, I was able to catch a glimpse of a female, not my aunt, in more-than-just-close proximity to Herbie. She was my aunt and uncle's next-door neighbor. After advancing closer it became clear that this was no laundry function I had ever before witnessed.

Herbie was kissing this woman and massaging several of her lady-parts. She didn't seem to mind. What was most mystifying was how any woman could find Herbie attractive enough to do anything more than hold her nose in his presence. But, as I was beginning to learn, there is no account-ing for taste, and desperate people do desperate things. The proof was in Lottie's marriage to this slob in the first place.

I watched them for several minutes, and when I became disgusted enough, I made my presence known.

"Helping you hang the sheets, is she?" I inquired. They couldn't see me because the wind had died down, even though Herbie obviously hadn't.

"Who's that?" he shouted.

He got his answer when I did a peek-a-boo, revealing my face through the sheets hanging between us.

"Hank, what are you doing here?" he asked, his face redder than the lady's underwear he clutched in his right hand.

"Taking down some laundry. And what are you taking down? You should be ashamed of yourself, Uncle Herb," I said, "and you, Mrs. Mitnitsky, are not very fussy."

I now know that Ruth Mitnitsky had inherited a considerable sum after her husband's passing. That could possibly have triggered the diddling episode, since Herb was in constant need of ways to fund his gambling addiction.

"Please don't tell Lottie," he begged.

"I won't," I replied, "and not because I'm protecting you. But do this again, and you might not like the results."

At the time, I wasn't sure how I would carry out that threat, but my knowledge of pyrotechnics might become part of it.

Chapter 19 • No Day at the Beach

"My life is like a stroll on the beach... as near to the edge as I can go."

-Thoreau

On a warm, mid-week, early summer afternoon, my buddies Marty Rose and Bob Broke (whom we all call "Gopher") and I are off for a day of fun. We stand in the forward section of the nearly deserted lead subway car, noses pressed against the seldom-cleaned streaked glass, optimistically anticipating our arrival at Brighton Beach station. The 'D' train, from an early vintage of subway cars on the BMT division, with its cane seats, hanging leather straps and ceiling fans, will take us to frolic in the sand and surf.

From our Crown Heights Brooklyn neighborhood, to the ultimate destination: Bay 5, Brighton Beach—affectionately known as the *Kosher Coney Island*, the trip costs a miserly fifteen cents. I'm reminded of the first time I rode this train to the beach, and the not-so-pleasant events that ended that day, including a police search to locate a bewildered and lost child.

Marty is busy reading an ad for *Mum Mist* adorning the wall, boasting that it now contains hexachlorophene. This prompts him to sniff each of his armpits, regretting that he's forgotten to apply that very product before leaving home.

The aging train rumbles though dark corridors buried deep beneath the streets of Brooklyn, palely illuminated by flickering incandescent lights. Suddenly, as if newly born, the car is saturated in blinding sunlight as it emerges from the tunnel onto an exposed section of track. Church Avenue station is the first stop not enclosed by burrowed earth and concrete. It's from this point that our train rides exclusively in open air on its way to its terminus at Stillwell Avenue

As the senior member of this motley group, somehow having survived to my seventeenth birthday, I'm the leader of the pack. We pause on the splintered boardwalk steps to survey the beach in search of ogle targets. When the appropriate site is selected, we haul our limited beach gear and deposit it on the sand, in a location midway between the surf and the boardwalk.

Gopher, with a rodential face and rotund body, is a little self-conscious as he slips down his jeans to reveal oversized red swim trunks. He looks around to see if anyone notices, and is relieved when no onlookers are detected. Marty's beach attire resembles something out of the *Museum of Bathing*, and his blissful unawareness of this fact allows him to be completely comfortable with himself. I hold in my stomach, as my bathing trunks are revealed for the first time. My early season tan is in sharp contrast with my buddies' ghostlike complexions.

Upon spotting her settling in with two of her friends, I'm immediately smitten as she bends over to straighten their blanket. She is slightly *zaftig*, which, in her two-piece bathing suit, works very much to her advantage. I'm unable to avert my gaze, but whenever she turns toward me I look away, pretending to be lost in thought.

Her friends are somewhat average looking and have the facial characteristics of members of my own tribe; not so the blond, blue-eyed, freckled *Goyisha* goddess.

I appeal to Marty and Gopher to move our stuff closer to the earthy treasure trove in order to better serve our romantic interests. They give the girls the once-over. Like me, they fancy only the blond.

A conversation breaks out over the din of Marty's portable radio, loyally tuned to WNEW. We hear Ella Fitzgerald's rendition of *The Very Thought of You* faintly in the background.

"Like she's going to give us a second look," opines Marty, not known for having the best self-image.

"Not us," I correct. "Me."

"In your dreams, Hank," Gopher chimes in.

"Dig this," I say, pointing to my crotch at what appears to be a rather substantial package of manhood.

"What did you do, stuff a potato in your bathing suit? I know that ain't all you. I've seen you in the pool," says Gopher, referring to our high school boys-only swim class, featuring nude bathing.

"You think I would do something as obvious as stuffing my crotch to impress a girl?" I challenge, with an unhideable smirk.

"Yes we do," Gopher and Marty answer in unison.

"Well, not all of us are hung like Marty over here, and sometimes nature could use a little assistance."

Marty blushes over the well-known fact that he was endowed by his creator with an unequal John Thomas.

"Shall we move closer to their blanket, or not?" I forcefully suggest.

"Alright," they reluctantly agree, having little confidence that this foray will lead to anything productive.

Marty and Gopher haphazardly drop their towels within a few feet of the target, but I, somewhat more meticulous, bend to straighten out my towel. It is richly embroidered with the words "Gay Cock Inn" with a rooster just below the gold lettering.

Titters began to break out in the surrounding area. Gopher and Marty look around see where the frivolity is coming from. I ignore the laughter, which becomes more widespread, and includes the vocal timbres of both genders. The girls on the blanket point to us and break into uproarious laughter. Marty and Bob examine themselves for embarrassing possibilities, but find nothing that could have engendered that kind of outburst.

Finally, curiosity gets the best of me. I need to know why the normal beach sounds of pounding surf and gentle rustling breezes have been replaced by those resembling a pack of hyenas in mating season. I realize that I might be the only soul in Brighton Beach that isn't laughing, my two companions having now joined the chorus.

"What is so funny?" I demand to know, which brings even more laughter from my comrades.

"Shall we tell him?" Gopher asks, "or should we let him discover it on his own?"

A debate breaks out as to what is the proper etiquette in situations of an unusual nature such as this.

"We owe it to Hank to tell him," Marty argues.

"But it's much more fun to let him discover that he might be the biggest *putz* in Brighton Beach history," counters Gopher.

Realizing that something has gone terribly awry, I finally look down to discover that my artificial enhancement is no longer in its intended place. I pat the back of my bathing suit and quickly understand why I might now have a larger audience than Soupy Sales.

"Schmuck," yells Gopher between bouts of hysterics. "You're supposed to keep the potato in the front."

I survey the beach for a parting of the sea so that I can disappear into it. "Where is Moses when you need him most?" I cry.

All I can do at this moment is run toward the shore. I obviously can't remain here fidgeting with my bathing trunks in order to remove the tuber, and hopefully I might be just lucky enough to drown in the surf.

It is impossible for me to return to the scene—the source of so much entertainment at my expense. My immersion in the icy water continues until there is no discernible difference between my complexion, and that of the ocean. Normally I would never have considered plunging into the unwelcoming Atlantic this early in the season, and there are but a few other die-hards in the surf to keep me company.

Hours go by and my friends' curiosity as to my whereabouts and condition have piqued. My wallet and clothing are still on my beach towel following my hasty retreat. I'm hoping my friends realize that I can't leave the beach without their help. I spot them heading down toward the shore to search for me. Marty discovers me low in the surf. Because of my water-slicked hair, my ears stand out even more than usual, which might be aiding in my discovery.

"Okay, Hank. You can come out now, your girlfriend has already left the beach," sings Marty.

"Make sure you take the potato with you, so you can have it for next time," taunts Gopher.

"V-ver-ry f-f-u-nny," my shivering voice replies.

I indicate my aversion to returning to our towels because I can't face the crowd. "C-could y-you g-get my s-stuff and m-meet me up on the board-walk at Bay 7?" I beg.

"What's it worth to you, potato boy?" teases Gopher.

"J-just m-meet me at the P-pizza Sh-shack in five m-minutes, and s-stop b-being a w-wise-ass."

Chapter 20 • We Wuz Robbed

"Get your facts first, then you can distort them as you please."

-Mark Twain

We're back on terra firma, heading toward the boardwalk, and far enough from Bay 5 to avoid my 'admiring' public. I slip my jeans on over my soaking wet trunks, bundle myself up in my fancy towel and hope that the remaining sun will bring my body back from a temperature measureable only on the Kelvin scale.

"What should we do now," asks Marty.

"It's too early to go home. Let's get some pizza and head over to Coney Island for the penny arcade," I suggest. It's a miracle that they still look to me for leadership.

We down four slices each of reheated, pizza-resembling cardboard, a few sodas and some soft ice cream. We are, after all, growing boys. After that elegant repast, we head west on the boardwalk toward our Coney Island destination, *The Pavilion of Fun.*

After throwing many coins into the various slots at the arcade we come to the realization that our funds have become mostly exhausted.

"Hey, I don't know if I have enough money for the subway," I exclaim.

"I'm broke," says Gopher, smiling, his two front pockets stretched inside out to verify his statement."

"How are we going to get home," Marty wonders, out loud.

"Easy," I offer. "We go to the police station and tell them we were robbed."

"Then what?"

"Simple. The cops will have no choice but to put us on the train. We ride home for free!"

This seems like a cunning plan, and wins quick acceptance.

We're lost in conversation about nubile girls and baseball, two subjects that dwarf all others in importance to us. It's not long before we arrive at the 60th precinct on West 8th Street, eager to tell our story to what we hope will be a sympathetic member of the Coney Island constabulary.

"Let me do the talking," I insist, as we pass though a pair of tall wooden doors.

Upon entering the building we're greeted by the desk sergeant, whose nametag reads "William Wierzejewski." He's as wide as the desk in front of him.

"Can I help you, boys?" he asks, his voice echoing under the tall ceilings in the 19th century station house.

"Yes," I answer, my voice cracking as I speak. "We just got robbed…"

"Yeah, down on the beach," Marty chimes in – drawing my icy stare.

"Okay," he says. "Why don't you boys have a seat on the bench over there and I'll get an officer to take your personal information."

After submitting our names, addresses and phone numbers to a uniformed cop not much our older than we are, we sit on the hard oak bench. A worried countenance appears on each of the three about-to-become juvenile delinquents.

"Did he say statements?" Marty queries, "Or statement? Singular or plural?" now cognizant of the fact that we might each have to give testimony.

Detective Sergeant O'Sullivan quickly removes any doubt, after appearing from behind a glass-paneled door, marked 'Interrogation.' He wears a white shirt with an open collar, from which a tie from an earlier era extends. "Mr. Robert Broke. Come this way please."

As Gopher disappears behind the door, with only the wide silhouette of his bulk showing through the translucent glass, the two remaining "victims" look at each other with hideously frightened expressions.

"This was your idea, genius," Marty reminds me.

"Shhhh. Do you want them to hear you?" I caution.

We sit back on the bench and stare out into space, amid the din of continuously ringing telephones. There isn't much to look at. Police stations are not noted for their interior decorating. An occasional glance our way from Sgt. Wierzejewski produces spasms of fear in the two of us.

"What's taking them so long in there?" wonders Marty.

"Maybe they're torturing him for information," I suggest, half believing it.

We listen for anguished screams that never come.

Marty is called next for interrogation, neither of us having seen Gopher emerge.

After what seems like a school year, the door opens and the detective stands in the doorway, beckoning for me to enter the room.

"Where's Marty and Gopher, I mean Bob?" I inquire of Sgt. O'Sullivan, while complying with his request for my presence behind the mysterious door.

"They'll be fine," assures the detective, in his 'police' accent. "We're just keepn' 'em in a little room for a while." Seemingly, all cops are required to speak in this voice.

It's now my turn. I walk the slow stride of the condemned, envisioning a darkened room with a bright lamp that would be shining in my eyes as I give testimony.

To my partial relief, no lamp appears. I sit down on a stool not designed for comfort.

"Now, Henry, Katz is it?"

"Yes, Katz"

"Jewish name, Katz?"

"Yes, but why..."

"Henry, you say you were robbed down at the beach, is that correct?"

"Yes, detective, down at Bay 12."

"Who were these alleged poipetratahs? Were they colored, Hispanic, Chinese, or what?" How many were they?" asks O'Sullivan, in rapid-fire succession.

"Excuse me. Poipetratahs?"

"Yeah, poipetratahs. People who commit crimes. Poip-a-tray-tahs."

I eventually translate the word from *Copese* to English. "Well, there were about 8 guys, some of them looked Puerto Rican or maybe Italian," I answer.

"Did they carry any weapons: knives, chains, bats?"

"Yeah, hey all had weapons of some kind, and their debs had weapons, too."

"So, let me see if I got this straight. Yous was attacked on the beach by a bunch of Latin types who were all armed, and their girlfriends were with them?"

"Correct." I affirm.

"And did they come from the east, the west, from the boardwalk?

"They came from under the boardwalk."

"Henry, I'm afraid your story doesn't match what was told to us by your two pals. I have their testimony right here," states the detective, pausing to focus his cold gray eyes on my scared shitless face. My squirms do not go unnoticed. He waits a full minute before continuing his interrogation, the whole time never removing his gaze from my frightened eyes.

"As a matter of fact, none of these statements agree. Now why did yez come in here with this bullshit story about bein' robbed? Giving false testimony is a very serious offense. What if we sent a radio car out to look for these so-called attackers? What if we arrested a bunch of *Spics* who were just out for a good time with their girlfriends? How would you feel if they spent the night in a cell, because of a story you made up?"

I can taste that cardboard pizza sickeningly mixed with bile as O'Sullivan lifts the phone and begins dialing.

"Mrs. Katz?" asks the sergeant, followed by a pause.

"Sgt. Frank O'Sullivan – Coney Island police."

My mother's reaction forces the sergeant to hold the phone away from his ear to avoid cochlear damage, while I hear and appreciate her every word.

"Sorry to disturb you, Mrs. Katz, but we have your son Henry here at the station…"

"What did he do now?" most of planet Earth could hear her ask.

"Him and his friends came in here with a cock and bull story about bein' robbed. This is a very serious matter," he informs her, holding the mouthpiece close and partially covering the earpiece with his massive left hand."

Despite the sergeant's attempt at quelling the earsplitting sound, her reaction "Let the bum spend a night in jail. That should teach him a lesson," can be heard right through the makeshift sound muffler.

The detective whispers something into the phone, then says "good bye" to Mrs. Katz.

"What have you got to say for yourself —wasting police time; falsely accusing someone of robbery?"

"I'm really sorry Detective," I utter, as his my eyes well up with tears. "It was a dumb thing to do. We spent all our money and hoped that you would put us on a train if you thought we were robbed. It was a stupid idea."

"Your mother thinks you should spend the night in a cell."

"My mother is not well. She doesn't mean it. She loves me. Please don't lock us up," I beg.

"If that's love, what does she say about people she can't stand?" O'Sullivan wonders out loud. "If we stick yez in a cell, you'd be sharing it with a pervert, a murderer or an arsonist, because that's what's in our three cells at the moment. Ok. Get the fuck out of here, and don't get in any more trouble today, hear?"

I exit the room, wiping the dripping perspiration from my face, and practically crawl into the large hall where Marty and Gopher are already waiting. Needless to say, I am not welcomed with open arms.

"Great plan, Hank," says Gopher, his sentiment echoed by Marty.

"Yeah, it was a crazy idea, which I might add, you both agreed to," I remind them.

"Ok, Einstein, how do we get home now?" demands Gopher.

"Well, we could try another police station," I suggest.

Chapter 21 • It Ain't Rocket Science

"You can't ask your pharmacist to stock larger quantities of potassium nitrate because you want to make a bigger rocket."

-Kary Mullis

Teddy Finkle's knock comes at precisely four p.m. You can set your watch by his punctuality. I open the door to see him standing there, clutching a wrinkled brown paper bag, while singing his own rendition of *In the Still of the Night.* He sounds nothing like the Five Satins. In fact, he doesn't sound like even one Satin, polyester, maybe, but definitely not satin. Though his voice benefits somewhat from the hallway echo, it is basically beyond salvation.

I hastily pull him into my folks' apartment, because without the echo, Teddy has no further incentive to sing. As I do, Teddy takes a final look around to ensure that he has not been followed. If he hadn't wanted to call attention to himself, why would he stand outside my door baying like a wounded hyena?

Teddy bears a close resemblance to Alfred E. Newman. But, unlike the Mad Magazine mascot, Teddy worries constantly—that his antics might be reported to his mother, known to be a strict disciplinarian. It is not unusual for her to haul off and give him a *chhmall* when she believes he acts inappropriately.

"*Chhmal*" is a *Yiddish* word meaning a backhand smash to the *punim* (face), mostly to embarrass, but if delivered with enough power is capable of causing disfigurement. Ana Finkle, whose body resembles that of a Bulgarian soccer star, is capable of administering such a blow. The constant threat of becoming the *chhmalee* keeps her son in line, at least while he's at home, which, understandably, is as little as possible.

Teddy lives in the shadow of his successful older brother, who met his unfortunate demise at the young age of twenty-seven. Teddy has dwelled in that darkness from his earliest recollection. The elder sibling, after a naval tour of duty, made a killing on Wall Street when he was in his mid-twenties. Everyone in my circle suspects the Finkle Family of being mob connected, but we are unsure of exactly what that means.

Teddy's brother was not able to enjoy, for very long, the fruits of his success. During a two-week reserve duty stint at Guantanamo, he slipped on a banana peel while inspecting the officers' dining facility. He did an almost complete midair flip, landing in a vat of rotting guava, giving new meaning to the term "officers' mess." He sank to the bottom almost instantly, with the opaque mire rendering him completely invisible. He was at first reported AWOL. The Shore Patrol canceled his arrest warrant only after a civilian staffer became sick from the vat's stench and discovered the body as he attempted to dump the putrid contents into Guantanamo Bay.

Teddy's arrival as the newest member of the Finkle household was, to say the least, inconvenient. Ana had been looking forward to retirement from child rearing. As parents in middle age, Ana and Israel Finkle had long forgotten how to raise a teen-aged boy. Ana never ceases to heap praise on her successful, departed *mensch*, while contrasting the two. "If you could study like your brother; if you could get grades like your brother; if you could get into Yale like your brother; if you can earn money like your brother; if you could be like your brother—he should rest in peace."

This was done in the presence of Teddy's friends, heightening his feelings of embarrassment and inadequacy.

Teddy holds his brother in the deepest reverence, and always refers to him as 'Brother.' None of our clique knows Teddy's sibling's given name, but we think it might actually be "Brother."

One of Teddy's more annoying and disgusting traits is that thing he does with his phlegm. I'm reminded of this lovely trait as Teddy pulls out a handkerchief that might hold the world's record for number of times used without laundering. I once made a note to check the *Guinness Book* to confirm this, but never got around to it. I prepare myself for the all-too-familiar sound of Teddy snorting the offensive effluvia from his nose, and lodging it in his throat, where it's either swallowed, or expectorated. The appearance of the fetid rag indicates that he's preparing to do the latter.

"Did you get the stuff?" I ask.

With his familiar Alfred E. Newman grin, Teddy raises the rumpled bag, dangles it before my eyes and gives the thumbs up sign. I grab it from his two fingers and we head for my room. Teddy pushes his way in. I forgot to mention the little surprise that I had rigged to the old *Webcor* tape recorder. It triggers when the door to my room is opened. The air fills with a blood-curdling scream coming from every speaker in the apartment. Teddy practically jumps out of his shoes at this unexpected aural assault.

I calm him down, and explain he can avoid the trap by turning the doorknob counter clockwise, instead of the reverse, to enter the room. Teddy regains his composure and begins laughing hysterically picturing my mother opening that door. I pop a stack of 45's onto the changer. Teddy sits on an old leather hassock while I dump the bag's contents out onto a small table, exposing three jars of colored powder: one black; one white; one yellow.

"How much did this cost us?" I ask.

"Three bucks."

"For all this?"

"For all this," he confirms. He has just returned from Canal Street where he has a connection to obtain sulfur, charcoal and chemically pure potassium chlorate (KCLO3). Teddy was acquainted with my past experience at Chen Chemical. Unlike the drugstore variety, this version, when haphazardly mixed, has the potential to become explosive. It also makes a respectable rocket fuel.

"Ah found mah threel…awwwwwn Blueberry Heel," wailes from the record changer.

I pay Teddy a dollar fifty for my share, plus fifteen cents for one half of the subway fare, even though I'm positive Teddy jumped the turnstile.

Teddy and I are the founders of **FSPIPP**, the *Flatbush Society for the Production and Ignition of Pyrotechnic Projectiles*. We are also its only members. We sank much of our hard-earned dough into the supplies needed to produce our product. Of course some of this inventory comes to us in less costly ways.

"Okay, what have we got now?" I ask.

Teddy begins reading from the newly modified inventory sheet in military fashion:

> **One, nine-inch pipe of the type 'lead,' slightly oxidized, found in a lot of the type 'vacant'**
>
> **One 4" x 4" wooden block of the type 'balsa,' liberated from a store of the type 'hobby'**
>
> **One roll of tape of the type 'electrical,' found in the tool chest of a man of the type 'father'**
>
> **One 6-Volt Ever-ready dry-cell battery of the type 'Heavy as a motherfucker,' actually purchased from a store of the type 'hardware'**
>
> **One can of metallic spray paint, of the type 'accidentally dropped in Teddy's bag'**

The rest of the list includes: 400 inches of bell wire, 'donated' by the Telephone Company—from the back of one of their green trucks parked out on the street, assorted items such as metal washers in graduated sizes; an emery cloth, metal shears; fine sandpaper, shaping knife, metallic aluminum paint (all obtained by Teddy out of the generosity of the hardware store proprietor while I was purchasing the dry cell); some empty cans; a Morse Code sender device, borrowed from their high school science lab; parts of several erector sets accumulated over the years. Some of those items were actually handled by 'Brother' himself. Completing the list of goods in our possession was a fine mortar and pestle set, left on the prescription counter by a careless pharmacist.

With Teddy's acquisition of the three chemicals, our inventory is complete. We are now ready to put those fine materials to use, and construct our first serious rocket. I envision it standing proudly on its launching pad, patiently waiting as the countdown draws closer to ZERO, anticipating the trigger that will send it streaking into the heavens.

Teddy mixes the three chemicals with the mortar and pestle in accordance with a formula I devised, without the slightest hint of understanding what he's doing. Creating an explosive is easy for me, but I'm not quite sure how to make this chemical mixture work as a fuel. After a little trial-and error, we will know soon enough. Isn't that how all great things get discovered?

While Teddy combines the potentially explosive mixture, a task I gladly turned over to him, I assemble the main rocket parts.

I momentarily bask in the glory of the previous night, when Joanne Katkin, the *Neighborhood Poster Child for Nymphomania*, paid me a visit. My concentration is interrupted when I notice and become alarmed at the vigorous pressure Teddy is applying as he mixes the powder. This material is highly volatile, when triturated —sort of like my mother.

"What are you fucken nuts?" I shriek, which, by the way, is not to suggest that Teddy is cohabitating with the mentally ill.

"Why? What's the matter?" he asks, all the while continuing to mix with the same gusto.

"Be gentle with that stuff," I warn. "If you rub it too hard, it will go off."

Teddy laughs in his typical imbecilic manner pointing to his crotch, making the obvious sexual reference.

"No, I mean it. This shit can go off at any time. I actually sleep in this room, and I expect a bed to still be here when I do. I have also grown especially fond of the walls."

Asking Teddy to be gentle is the equivalent of expecting a lioness to wipe her mouth with a napkin after each tiny forkful of gazelle. But he does heed the warning and begins mixing the powders with a little more regard to self-preservation.

We finally finish compounding and the resulting concoction is a muted yellowish-gray, slightly crystalline from the potassium chlorate. I sandpaper the balsa block into something remotely resembling the tip of a small howitzer shell, and apply aluminum paint to it. It now matches the color of the rocket body that was earlier sanded to remove its rough edges and smooth its oxidized surface. I wedge the head into one end of the pipe. It enters reluctantly.

Teddy looks up and makes another sexual reference. He has been assembling the launching platform from the many erector set pieces, again attempting to follow in Brother's footsteps. What it lacks in color coordination is made up in sturdiness, and it appears worthy of its intended task.

Strips of electrical tape are used to form the letters **FSPIPP**, which will adorn the side of the rocket. This will enable the finder (who knows how far distant?) to acknowledge the maker of this fine projectile. Teddy's mixture is ready for pouring into the open end of the pipe, and using a funnel, he fills it without spilling a drop. Steps are required to keep the charge in place. A wire, bent into a U, is inserted so that it makes contact with the charge—open ends out. Teddy makes a charge 'shaper' out of the decreasing sized metal washers that will force the escaping exhaust through the tiny opening of the last washer.

Our Amateur Rocketeer book suggested that shaping the charge could increase the rocket's thrust. The remainder of the U protrudes past the smallest washer. At launch time, each end of the U will be connected to a long length of bell wire (Thank you 'Ma'). This is the basis of the launch ignition system. The wires' other ends, hopefully at a safe distance, will hook up to the Morse sender and the dry cell terminals. Depressing the sender will complete the circuit. The U is expected to attain sufficient temperature to ignite the fuel.

Crude fins made smooth with electrical tape are attached, and the rocket is now complete.

So, here she is, standing tall on her erector set launch pad. We and the missile will wait impatiently for the day when we can get a lift out to spacious *Floyd Bennett Field*, where there are hardly any people. There she will be sent on her maiden voyage, which, if successful, will be her only voyage. We are eager to watch her slowly disappear, akin to how I feel about my sister.

Teddy is impatient. He hints about wanting to try a test launch from my bedroom. I convinced him that it is not the soundest of ideas. Still Teddy continues looking out the window, trying to spot a path the rocket could take that wouldn't hit anything major. He conveniently forgets that we're located in the midst of a huge housing complex.

"You remember the last such experiment," I remind him, "when we put a test rocket into that sand box…"

"Oh yeah, the one that used to be in the J building area." he acknowledges.

We had used the cement sides of this sandbox to prop up a 'launching tube" within which was wedged one of our earlier experiments. It was a missile made of cardboard and filled with a fuel whose reaction to heat was somewhat unpredictable. The tube was a lead chem-lab sink stopper, recently 'donated' by my bald chemistry teacher, aptly named Mr. Bush, who was absent on the day of the donation. The sandbox stood in a play area amid one of the ubiquitous courtyards in this densely populated complex.

Deluded by the belief that we were sophisticated in the art of fuse making, we attempted to launch the missile, using a fuse constructed of aluminum foil wrapped around a mixture of potassium chlorate and sulfur. We tested this as a fuse once, and were convinced of its ability to do the job. For safety sake (and safety was paramount when conducting experiments of this nature), we made the fuse two feet long. The length gave us sufficient time to ignite it, and hastily withdraw to an observation point behind a brick wall.

As with all great scientific endeavors, unplanned events can occur. Unpredictably the fuse became extinguished within about six inches of the propellant.

But we knew that science must go on.

I convinced Teddy to re-light the fuse at its new, shorter and more perilous length. It was a windy evening, and one match after another gave its life to the cause, until finally one stayed lit, long enough to restart the fuse. Teddy ran toward the wall, behind which I was securely nestled, as the flashing vaporous trail darted quickly toward the rocket. He barely made it in next to me when a most deafening explosion rocked the courtyard, making significant alterations to the play area—namely ridding it of that ugly sandbox.

"Well, I don't think we want to try that with this baby," I say.

"You never like to have any fun," he answers.

"It'll be loads of fun at the 71st precinct," I warn, "and even more fun in Creedmoor,"—a reference to the infamous state mental hospital.

Teddy suggests that we take a small amount of the compound and see what happens when heat is applied to it. The substance isn't confined in a tight container, so I don't perceive it to be dangerous.

"So, the hell with it," I declare. "Let's test a small quantity." The only vessel at our disposal is the mortar, which is much too nice to be used for this experiment.

I go into the living room to procure one of my mother's ashtrays that she had removed from the popular *Lindy's of Sheepshead Bay*, one of the many souvenirs to which she felt entitled, as a patron of the establishment.

I place the ashtray on my bedroom floor. "Let me light it. Let me light it," cries Teddy, like a child at a birthday party.

"Here, go ahead, you pyromaniac," I say throwing him a book of matches.

He bends over the ashtray, which has about a tablespoon of the leftover mixture. He prepares to light the compound while it's directly under him. Apropos of this, Johnny Cash's *Ring of Fire* plops down on to the record stack. I yank Teddy back just as he's about to drop the match into the ashtray, landing him on his derriere. "We'll worry about brain damage later," I think, as I've just saved what, to Teddy, was a far more important part of his anatomy.

There's a brilliant flash, as a miniature Hiroshima appears out of what was formerly an ashtray. The room fills from floor to ceiling with smoke.

As it rises, I spot a small fire in the floor. I am alert enough to throw Teddy's jacket on it, quickly extinguishing it. With both the window and door closed, the smoke has nowhere to go, except into our lungs. We begin choking.

Our dilemma is manyfold. If we open the window, there will be an outpouring of smoke, which might prompt someone to call the fire department. We would prefer to avoid that. Opening the bedroom door will flood the other rooms with smoke. This is also not very good, and it still doesn't solve the problem of removing the smoke from the premises.

Our eyes tear as pungent sulfur dioxide and other pollutants fill our lungs. Luckily, most of the other apartments are empty of occupants in this working-class neighborhood. Eventually, however, someone will be sure to notice the smoke.

"It seems to me," I tell Teddy, "that our only hope is create a diversion."

"What do you have in mind?" he asks, his curiosity piqued.

"Oh, I was thinking that we (meaning he) could start a small, harmless fire in one of the trash cans outside, somewhere up the street. Any fire vehicles or cop cars arriving in the neighborhood responding to some nosy neighbor's report of smoke would have to focus their attention on this fire."

Teddy thinks the idea is brilliant. He can't wait to get his grubby little hands on some matches, having benefited little from the previous learning experience.

We hastily withdraw from the choking air and quickly slam the door shut. The hard whack of the door against its frame starts the *Webcor* going. I'm not finding this to be pleasurable as I race against time to close all of the other doors in the apartment, to keep the smoke as confined to my bedroom as possible. If someone looking up to my second floor window from the street, sees smoke and hears screams reminiscent of King Kong in heat, we could be in a serious predicament.

"I must not panic. I must NOT PANIC. I MUST NOT PANIC," I chant, as I desperately try to calm down—not an easy feat given the circumstances. I enter my folks' bedroom and pull the doors closed behind me. I inspect the room for telltale smoke. It seems to have escaped the noxious odor. Out of the window I spot Teddy dashing up the street with a gasoline canister in his hand. Finkle is as resourceful as a Warner Bros. cartoon character, seemingly plucking anything he needs from thin air.

I go through the rest of the apartment, and I'm reasonably assured that the smoke damage is confined to only my room. I hunt for the large floor fan, hidden in some off-season place. This is a three-bedroom apartment with many closets. It shows up in the fourth place I look, as the wail of fire engine sirens become audible. I try to keep cool amid the cacophony of Fire Company No. 7, the screaming *Webcor* with Elvis warning me not to step on his shoes.

With a handkerchief around my face to cover my mouth and nose, I drag the fan into the smoky room. Nervous hands pull the door shut, rip the *Webcor* plug out of the wall, finally quieting the booby trap screamer, causing Elvis to murmur "Bloooo Sueeeeeeede shu…" as the song winds down to a premature halt. Holding my breath, I tug at the window in an effort to open it, planning to place the fan in front of it in the reverse position to suck out the smoke. With my luck, naturally the window is stuck. Three fingernails are sacrificed before it finally budges. I plug in the fan. In my panic I face the fan in the wrong direction forcing the smoke to blow inward. My homework scatters about the room in all directions.

Short words of Anglo-Saxon origin accompany my experience.

I finally get the fan turned around and so it can suck the smoke out of the room, and through the window. I observe a crowd gathering near my window, but they are not looking in my direction. "Say hallelujah, say thank you, Jesus," I declare.

Teddy appears at my bedroom door, with a shit-eating grin on that face that only a mother could love, but probably doesn't.

"Did you set a garbage can on fire? I asked. "I did see you with a gasoline can."

"Better." he says. "You know the Cadillac that colored guy leaves parked out here all the time?"

He was referring to Jerome, who comes around daily to visit his 'girls,' making no attempt to blend in seamlessly. Everyone in the neighborhood knows that car. It's a white convertible with leopard top, ermine seat covers, and gold grill with wire hubcaps to match—not easy to miss.

"You mean the *El Pimpo Brougham*?"

"Gone." says Teddy, with a wink.

We are, for the moment, saved.

Chapter 22 • Werner, Where Are You?

"A good rule for rocket experimenters to follow is this: always assume that it will explode."

-Astronautics, issue 38, October 1937

My mother has probably punched out and will return to the apartment at any moment. I give the place the sniff test and detect slight traces of the fumes that several hours earlier had totally saturated the apartment. I wonder if she'll notice. I decide to greet her in the courtyard, or more accurately, to intercept her.

"Hi Mom," I shout, seeming almost too glad to see her.

"Hello, son, what are you doing out here?"

"Just coming out to greet the best Mom in the world."

"Don't give me any of that bullshit," she says, "You never greet me coming home from work. What kind of trouble are you in, now?"

"Can't a kid just be happy to see his mother?" I sigh—crestfallen.

"Henry, I know you too well. What the hell is going on? And where is your sister?"

"Nothing's going on, Ma. And Sydney's at her friend Beth's. She's having dinner there, and speaking of food, is supper ready?"

She laughs at the absurdity that she could somehow have conjured up our supper while bussing back from her job.

"I have a great idea," I say. "You're tired. Worked hard. Had a long day. Why don't we go out for *Chinks* tonight? My treat."

"What are you, *mishuga*?" she asks. "I need to go upstairs, take off my shoes and relax for while, and then I'll make supper."

Realizing that it's already five fifteen, that food would not be on the table until at least six thirty, and that the practice of rocketry stimulates appetite, I whine, "But I'm hungry, Ma."

"You're hungry? *Leg Zaltz*, and *Fadray mir nischt in kopf.*"

This is Edie's typical response whenever I mentioned a craving for food. It means, 'Lick salt (so you can be thirsty as well as hungry), and stop bothering my head'. *Yiddish* is an amazing form of shorthand. It's not routinely spoken in the household, except to register a complaint, or utter an insult.

As I am unable to talk my mother into doing an about face and trudging off with me to Sing Wu, I reluctantly follow her upstairs. I stand in fear as she unlocks the door to our apartment. Her olfactory senses are working, detecting something that isn't quite right. At first it's a simple sniff or two. It then progresses to the bloodhound stage, where it becomes a series of deep nasal intakes in very rapid motion.

"I smell dynamite in here," she proclaims. "Henryyyyy, have you been playing with those stupid rockets, again? Are you trying get us evicted?

"What is the matter with you? Are you *mishuga*? Was your idiot friend Teddy here with you, today? Why don't you light rockets off in his house?"

There is nothing I can say that will, to Mom's satisfaction, end this interminable inquisition. I remain silent as her shrill voice cuts through me like new chalk on a blackboard. She threatens to enter my room, to fully investigate the source of the odor. My reactions are not quick enough to prevent her from turning the knob on my bedroom door. The booby trap, which I had thoughtlessly reconnected, is triggered, and Edie screams in reaction to the horrific torrent of sound emanating from my makeshift P.A. system.

I conclude that Mom won't be pleased when she recovers from her shock. It might even delay supper.

"Sorry," I meekly utter.

I take her by the arm and escort her into her bedroom, seeing to it that she lies down. I slip off her shoes and cover her legs with part of the chenille bedspread.

"Are you okay?" I ask.

Lying on the bed, staring blankly at the ceiling, she refuses to answer. I'm thinking how relieved I am that this is an evening my father works his second job. As I attempt to take leave of her, she suddenly snatches my hand; the sharp tips of her fingernails almost breaking the skin.

"Those rocket things need to be out of your room by tonight. I want those speakers disconnected. I want this house to be NORMAL. Do you HEAR ME?"

After all these years she still doesn't understand that normal is not a possibility for the Katz household. Still, I answer in the affirmative and meekly leave her bedroom.

My first instinct is to protect the investment of the *Flatbush Society For the Production and Ignition of Pyrotechnic Projectiles*. I draw warning labels designed to dissuade anyone determined to rid our dwelling of these dangerous elements. Using oak tag and my best India inks, I carefully construct several placards, warning that the slightest movement of these highly unstable materials might cause them to explode, and under NO circumstance should they be touched, dusted, breathed on, etc.

Acknowledging that my speaker system got me in trouble twice this day, I make an intelligent decision to disassemble the booby trap mechanism. The thought of disconnecting all of the speakers seems inimical to me. They're way too much fun. For example, they can be set up as microphones, and when hooked up to the input jack on the *Webcor*, can record conversations anywhere in the apartment. They can be used to broadcast phony radio messages, as was the case several evenings back when it was announced that school would be closed for three days due to a teachers' conference. Why live in a place bereft of these enhancements?

Somehow I manage to survive the next few days, and the weekend arrives. Teddy has made an arrangement with his sister Eva (no, her name is not 'Sister') to drive us out to Floyd Bennett Field. She drops us off at Avenue V and Flatbush Avenue. Eva asks us what's in the large shopping bag. We tell her it's kite-making material. That seems quite reasonable.

She tells us to have fun and then drives away to her house in Mill Basin, not far from the drop-off point. It's a gray autumn day, and the field is the muted color of straw that seems to go on forever.

Teddy and I scout the area for a site we think will be safe. We're convinced that the missile has the potential to travel miles. At first we ponder the possibility of aiming it at the Marine Park Golf Course. But we're overtaken by a bit of good judgment and decide to pick a direction where the missile is unlikely to hit anyone. The trajectory is set for due east, which will take it in the direction of Broad Channel. It will have to travel about a mile and a half if it's to clear the field and plunge into the drink.

Our excitement mounts as we set up the launch platform, and string the fuse wire that will carry the spark to ignite the missile's fuel. A few drops of rain begin falling. We remain undaunted by the knowledge that even a monsoon cannot prevent this epic event from taking place.

The projectile stands proudly on its Erector Set launch pad, its nose tilted slightly to the east. The sending device lies in a ditch about a hundred yards from where our baby stands. The foxhole-like depression will provide protection on the odd chance our creation explodes as it attempts its rise into space.

The countdown begins, although there is absolutely no reason for one.

"Thirty…"

The rain picks up a little and the wind, typical for this area, whips against our faces, driving the droplets into us like sharp little nettles. A gaggle of Canadian Geese is seen flying overhead. We know they are Canadian Geese because instead of squawking as they whiz by, they crow "Aye, Aye, Aye." We hope that the birds will not be in the path of our missile when it defies gravity and lifts majestically into the air.

"Fifteen, fourteen…"

My hand waits nervously on the trigger. Teddy indicates his disappointment that he won't be pushing the sender key to make the spark on the other end. Begrudgingly I signal Teddy to also place his finger on the key so that we can share the credit for the making of this model missile milestone.

We can almost hear a drum roll as the countdown continues.

"Two, one, zero." Our fingers simultaneously push down on the key. I locate the launching platform with my twenty-power binoculars. We wait in anticipation, unsure of how long it will take for one hundred yards of bell wire to heat a thin filament at the launch pad. After waiting what seems like eternity, we notice smoke gushing from the rocket's base. A steady stream of fiery exhaust accompanies the gray smoky billow. It reminds me of the Army rocketry films we'd seen on the *MovieTone News*. In those documentaries, ignition took place, thrust was built, slowly at first—but then thunderously, followed by a slow rising, as if pulled by a hidden wire overhead. But that's where the similarity ends. Unlike the Army missile that escapes its pad, leaving a plume of vapor to follow it into the heavens, ours sits there immobile until its fuel is entirely spent; and then topples over.

Smoke continues to escape from its tail, in an ever decreasing volume. We wait a good ten minutes to allow for the rocket to cool off, and sadly approach it. It is impossible for us to mask our disappointment. It is difficult to tell how much of the liquid streaming down our faces is rainwater and how much is tears.

With our shopping bag filled with the spent rocket and sundry equipment, we make the slow wet walk to the stop where the Flatbush Avenue Bus can carry two dejected rocket scientists back home.

Chapter 23 • Fools' Errands

"April 1. This is the day upon which we are reminded of what we are on the other three hundred and sixty-four."

-Mark Twain

Another April 1st rolls around. This is a big annual event for the Katz household, for it's the birthday of the entire family. It has become a big joke that all members of our clan share April Fools' Day as our common birthday. The odds that four members of the same family are born on the same month and day are astronomical.

Shopping bags litter the apartment, resulting from four family members having returned from E.J. Korvette with a gift for every other.

We gather around the dinette table, with its pink faux-marble top and rusting chrome legs, seated on tufted red leatherette chairs. Birthday gifts are piled on the top of the table, which Dad was supposed to have wiped clean with a sponge, but failed to complete satisfactorily. The smell of Mom's overcooked hamburgers, long ago consumed, still hangs in the air, as a testament to her thorough heating.

Edie runs a finger along an unoccupied portion of the table top, sending a look of scorn in her husband's direction. Sol, spotting her sneer along with her finger pointing at the grease mark, utters some pale excuse for failing to do his part.

Mom is ready to begin the gift exchange and shows zero tolerance for those who are not ready to participate.

"Okay," she shouts. "Time to open our presents. Henry? Where are you?"

I cannot fail to hear her clarion call, but at that moment I'm busy performing my daily—and sometimes even more frequent—onanistic ritual.

"In a second, Ma," I call out from behind the bathroom door, meaning it literally. It never requires much time for me to complete this task.

"What the hell were you doing in there all this time?" she asks as I emerge from my palace of pleasure with a reddened complexion.

Though two minutes is not exactly an epoch, it has been established that Edie's patience is not her long suit. She's either unfamiliar with, or chooses to ignore, the testosterone tidal flow generated by adolescent males.

"Sorry, Ma," I apologize, catching a knowing wink from my father.

Sydney has the honor of presenting the first gift. She extends a small package to Dad. He accepts it as if he's never before received a gift; overjoyed as he tears open the wrapper.

"*Oy Gevalt*," he exclaims. "A three cent stamp from British Guyana! How did you know I have been looking for this all over?" For a ten-year old, her numismatic prowess seems quite amazing, although she did have 'some' help from me.

He picks up his pudgy young child, hugging and kissing her profusely.

"Doesn't take much to satisfy this man," opines Edie, who is an expert on the subject.

The gifts are all distributed, and the obligatory "You shunta's" are echoed. None of the presents are worth very much, as the family struggles from paycheck to paycheck. We all appreciate the modest offerings as if they come from *Tiffany's*.

The most memorable presents went to Sydney and me, probably as compensation for the unwanted pajamas we each received the previous year, the year before, and the year before that. This time we've each received baseballs, signed by our chosen teams: She, the entire '67 Mets roster (they write small), while my ball has the signatures of most of the Yankee players on last year's team.

Since my sister and I root for rival teams (at least she believes that they are rivals), we rarely watch a game together, except for a rare meeting of the two teams in an exhibition game. We hold our baseballs in each other's faces, while I remind Sydney that her heroes lost one hundred and twenty games in their first season. That painful truth does not shake her faith.

"Well, at least I didn't switch teams when the Dodgers moved away," she reminds me, a miraculous observation from one of such a tender age.

"Well, na-na-na-na. In 1958, you didn't know a baseball from a matzo ball," I taunt. "On second thought, the way Mommy cooks matzo balls, no one could tell the difference."

Sydney also treasures a framed photo of heartthrob Tab Hunter, the object of her preadolescent fantasies, and who happens to be half Jewish. He also happens to make me fully nauseous.

To extend out our mutual birthdays celebration, Edie has planned for us to have an elaborate dinner at *Hung Lo* in Chinatown. I refer to that eatery as "Hung Well." All but little Sydney laugh each time I make that name substitution. For celebrating, any place is better than Mom's kitchen, which gave new meaning and spelling to the term "burned at the steak."

Here, the entire family can dine for about twelve bucks, including tip. To the Katzes, extravagance knows no bounds.

Sol begins looking for a parking spot just after our newly acquired, but previously owned, Chevy Wagon rolls off the Williamsburg Bridge. We're about a mile from Mott and Grand Streets.

This elicits a response from Edie, who suggests, "Why so close? Why not park in the Bronx so that we can have a good walk?"

Sol is notorious for taking the first available spot, coming from the notion of scarcity of all things. "Bird in the hand, Edie. Bird in the hand."

We hike toward the restaurant, as Edie frowns the entire way. I, on the other hand, spend the time checking out the ladies along the route. I'm particularly attracted to women of Asian extraction, maybe because none of them look anything like Katz family members.

We finally arrive at the restaurant almost thirty minutes after parking the car. It's before five, and *Hung Lo* is not even close to being filled to capacity. With a look that can kill, Edie points to the three parking spots practically right outside the restaurant's door.

"In China, he has to park," she snarls.

"I didn't think we'd get a spot," is offered as his defense.

"You never think we'll get a spot," she says, in disgust. Followed by, "That man. God, give me strength."

We're ushered to a table near the door. Edie rejects that location because it's too close to the entrance. She similarly refuses several other tables. Finally, the unsmiling manager points to a table in the rear. "But it's so close to the kitchen," moans Edie.

"Take it or leave it," says Mr. Hung in heavily accented English, or was it Mr. Lo?

"Let's just sit down and eat," I suggest.

Menus eventually appear before us after an extended wait, which doesn't go unnoticed by Edie. "A good tip they think they'll get from me?" is her comment.

Ah, the Chinese restaurant; a place for Jews to eat all the things God forbids within the home, but seems to have no problem with their consumption of pork and shrimp in a restaurant.

"The alleged God is good," I observe, inviting one large sneer from Edie. She's not exactly religious, but to hedge her bets, not blasphemous either.

"Watch your mouth in here," she warns. "You never know who's listening."

"Who cares?" I answer. "We don't know anyone in here."

"That may be true, but some people get upset when you talk about God that way."

Sol is too busy examining the menu to become involved in this discussion.

"Sol, you could say something to your son, also, you know."

"Edie, *lezem gayne* (leave him be)," says Sol the peacemaker. "We're here to eat and celebrate our birthday."

Mom mumbles under her breath while trying to make a selection for herself and Sydney, who, at eleven, is not considered mature enough to choose her own grub. Decisions are finally made and we are ready to order. Edie's eyes search for someone to service our table. She stops an Asian man wearing a grease stained smock, supporting a forty-pound bag of rice on one shoulder and carrying a bucket in his other hand.

"Are you our waiter?" she asks, based on the assumption that if you have a yellow complexion, you must be a Chinese waiter. This is met by a confused stare. The man disappears into the kitchen, without a reply.

"Probably some illegal alien," she comments. "Chinatown is full of them."

Sydney, Dad and I stare up at the ceiling, pretending we don't know who the woman is that's sitting at our table.

Minutes later, but in what Edie would have described as an eternity, a waitress, in her late teens, wearing a tight skirt, appears at the table, order book in hand.

"Do you know what you want?" asks the lovely young thing.

Mesmerized by a pair of perfect legs, I reply, "I know what I want." Dad and I are alone in our appreciation of the sentiment.

"Before we order, do you have any specials?" Edie asks.

"Sorry. We have a very extensive menu, and all of our items are shown. We don't offer specials."

"Okay, I'll have the roast pork *lo mein*. Does that come with anything?"

"Ma'am, if you look at the menu you will see that all of our entrees are served with soup and eggroll."

"Well, you don't have to be snippy…"

"Ma, she is not being snippy," I interrupt. "Just look at the Goddamn menu. She assumes that you can read, although I can't imagine why."

"Don't talk fresh to your mother," Dad admonishes.

"Can we just order our food?" demands Sydney.

Both 'adults' give the waitress their orders, changing their minds several times.

The Katzes appear to be the center of attention at this establishment, with all heads turned in our direction. Are we being loud and obnoxious, I wonder, and then answer my own question: "Is Moshe Dayan circumcised?"

Sydney inquires as to whether the eggs are really a thousand years old. At this point I suggest that the *previously-digested chicken* might be more to her liking.

"Ewwwww," she says, with an expression that goes with the reply.

Finally, in what may go down as the lengthiest ordering process in Hung Lo history, Miss Shapely-Legs disappears into the kitchen, shaking her head as she pushes open the double doors.

A few minutes go by, and three bowls of soup are placed on the table. Edie and Sydney will share. As a protective mother, she blows profusely on their egg drop soup to spare her young charge possible lip and tongue scalding. She attempts to place a spoon full of the gooey substance into her daughter's mouth. A look of revulsion appears on Sydney's face.

"I don't like it, Mommy."

"EAT IT ANYWAY," Edie commands.

Sydney asserts her defiance by putting her hands up to her face to block. Edie is determined to succeed, attempting to force the spoon past Sydney's tiny defensive hands. This results in a wad of egg drop glop flying through the air and landing on an unsuspecting patron about to put the front end of a pair of chopsticks into his mouth.

"SORRY," we shout in unison. We have all been here before.

The victim of the egg drop onslaught immediately requests another table, preferably as far from the Katz family as possible, and maybe even in a different restaurant.

Edie then tastes the soup and pronounces it COLD!

"Of course it's cold, Ma," I say. "You blew on it for practically a decade." Edie is not the only household member capable of exaggeration.

"MISS, MISS, THIS SOUP IS COLD."

If I were the waitress, I would probably be thinking, "I'll have the chef piss in it. That should warm it up."

A hot bowl of soup comes out, along with the entrees and eggrolls. Edie's ire has been provoked, as she now has to deal with soup and all the other courses. Surely, by the time she's ready to eat the rest, it too will have turned cold, and only a hernia operation without anesthesia could be worse than a tepid eggroll.

Despite the threats from Edie, including legal action, and possibly a phone call to the Immigration Service, the waitress refuses to take the entrees back.

Defiant Edie stands up and declares, "We're leaving."

A half-chewed piece of lobster Cantonese falls off my tongue, my mouth agape in disbelief.

When we have recovered our composure, we inform Edie that she may have over-reacted. Sydney chants, "But I'm still hungry."

The manager arrives at the table, smiling even less than in Edie's original encounter with him.

"Please leave restaurant," he demands. "You no pay. Just go."

Sol realizes that he has just scored a bargain; having devoured his dish as if in an eating contest. A free *egg foo yung* dinner? What could be better?

We exit the restaurant in what I hope will be in a dignified fashion. That hope is quickly dashed as Sydney is dragged kicking and screaming from her seat, strewn with the detritus of what might have been a wonderful birthday meal.

Chapter 24 • It's Alive!

"A flash of lightning illuminated the object and discovered its shape plainly to me; its gigantic stature, and the deformity of its aspect, more hideous than belongs to humanity, instantly informed me that it was the wretch, the filthy demon to whom I had given life."

-Mary Shelly

Francis N. Stein's head was a project from my sculpture class. He appears almost human, with a flesh-like color having been applied to his ceramic face, and hair from the barbershop floor, meticulously glued on. His face resembles that of a corpse, laid out at a wake, that elicits from the mourners the uncomfortable and inevitable, "…he seems so, so… lifelike."

Closets and drawers fly open, as a search begins for just the right garments to adorn the monster. The body, already constructed of old sheets stuffed with rags and newspaper, waits patiently to be dressed. A pair of realistic, gangrenous hands is attached to the wrists, supplied by a schoolmate whose father sells wax figures.

I am careful not to damage the speaker cone that is placed about chest high, and is covered with a tee-shirt, bloodied by Teddy Finkle's finger. He had unselfishly slashed his pinky with a razor blade (anything for the cause). Let us not forget to connect the speaker wires to the jack so that we can plug in our amp—another accoutrement to give our baby the power of speech, (or more precisely—the power of grunt.) It will be a lovely touch when the monster is presented to the judges.

We find little in the way of clothing from my room that will be appropriate for Frank. My father's closet will have to be the source of the monster's costume. Dad's wardrobe is far more suitable for clothing the monster than it is for clothing him. Dad won't miss the thirty-year-old slacks and still older shirt that I now pull from his closet. My father's slacks, though old, are neatly pressed, probably because they have been on the hanger since Moses' *Briss*. They will have to be put in the frayed condition consistent with what Frankenstein's monster would have worn at the time of his execution. I summon the faithful Lancelot to help in this endeavor.

The dog is not good for much, but he can shred garments with his teeth quite expertly. I dangle the slacks in front of the dog. He begins barking excitedly. He catches a pant leg in his mouth, and then shakes his head violently from left to right and right to left, as if wrestling with the mailman. His throat emits that playacting, mean, canine growl and he quickly rips the slacks and drowns them in drool—truly living up to his nickname.

Within minutes, this antique article of clothing has morphed into an unrecognizable rag. The shirt is given similar treatment. Teddy and I watch Lance transform it into ribbons of ruptured rayon. We hate to see the shirt, which has a design of mystical medieval symbols, so mercilessly destroyed.

Probably, if one were patient—lets say another fourteen hundred years—the Merlin look might come back into fashion.

We get the jaundiced head onto the body using a rolling pin, which inserts into the hollow head, stuffed for support with modeling clay—the other end of the pin is jammed between the shoulders. A pair of hiking boots and a patently ugly mackinaw, purchased only a few years earlier at *Klein's on the Square*, completes the outfit. Frank is now ready for his test walk.

Teddy and I grab the monster by the waist and leave the apartment. We take the elevator down one floor, hoping to meet an unsuspecting passenger waiting to get on at the lobby level. Anxious to test the creature's ability to strike terror into the heart of any observer that is likely to see it, we get our wish as Mrs. Ginsburg tries to board when the door opens. She is my next-door neighbor and knows Teddy and me quite well, each of us having babysat for her grandchildren from time to time.

"Hello, Henry. Hello, Teddy," she says. "And how are you Mr. Katz? You know, you don't look so good. Henry, has your father been to see a doctor?"

Once Mrs. Ginsburg is out of earshot, Teddy and I turn to one another and are unable to control our tears of laughter.

"Didn't exactly scare the shit out of her, did it?" Teddy asks.

"No," I reply, "and she will probably blab to everyone in the building that my father is near death, or worse."

We emerge into the courtyard with our hands supporting Frank from the rear while we each grab an arm, so that he can appear to wave to folks as they go by. It is so close to Halloween that people pay little attention. Just two young, pimply-faced punks, out for a walk with their toy monster.

Walking Frank is difficult, and he almost loses his head when Teddy, pulling out his infamous handkerchief, releases his grip causing the monster to keel slightly over.

We finally arrive at Kramer and Cooperberg's, the Jewish Delicatessen at Nostrand and Foster Avenues, where we plan to set up our test. It's early evening and the deli is packed. We observe mountains of cold cuts consumed by insatiable mouths of all ages. Orders of *French for the Money*, drowning in ketchup, appear ubiquitously in varying states of consumption. *Dr. Brown's Cel-Ray Tonic* bottles adorn nearly every table. Patrons all speak with mouths full, in a hundred conversations that occur simultaneously and independently.

Howie Kornbluth is at the grill, flipping *knishes*. A half-eaten hot dog sits on a plate near his workspace. His apron is painted with a gob of freshly spilled mustard. He spots us and nearly has a 'knish' himself when he sees Frank staring back at him. Howie is six-four, and hasn't had his big-growing year yet. But nature makes allowances; his brain hasn't had it either.

We laugh at the sight of this big *djlub* about to pass out from the shock of seeing what is perceived to be a standing cadaver.

"Teddy, grab an arm and wave it at the nice folks slobbering over their pastrami."

He obediently complies with my request. Others look up, nudging one another to glance in our direction. Some look as though they are going to be sick. We are not sure if it's Frank or the corned beef that's to blame.

"Well, I guess our boy is a success," Teddy exclaims, wiping his nose with a rag that could lose in a beauty contest with raw sewage.

We are satisfied that we have achieved the desired effect, and that we can proceed with our Halloween trip to Marlborough Dude Ranch, where Frank will surely win us a free weekend.

Chapter 25 • Rough Riders

"Have you ever noticed that anybody driving slower than you is an idiot, and anyone going faster than you is a maniac?"

-George Carlin

Saturday morning arrives, and four of us: Teddy, Marty, Billy and I, meet at the Newkirk Avenue station to begin a trip that will take us deep into the Poconos. There is panoply of equipment to be carried, including the hernia-inducing *Webcor* tape recorder. In addition, there are costumes, riding boots, and of course, Frank, who has been temporarily disassembled and placed in a valise. No one thinks of getting a taxi, so we plod our way down endless flights of subway stairs. Three of us pull out money for tokens.

Teddy is against the practice of actually paying to ride the subway, on religious grounds. He intends to leap the turnstile just as the train pulls in, carrying nearly eighty pounds of assorted luggage and equipment. After several moments of combined pressure from the group, he is convinced that saving fifteen cents is hardly worth requiring a truss.

We decide to regale our few weekend fellow passengers with some of our fabulous doo-wop.

"Hey, pipe down, over there, rotten teenage punks," yells one laborer type, failing to appreciate the quality of the entertainment.

Only after a fusillade of invectives and several threats of bodily harm do we actually cease and desist. Some people just don't appreciate quality.

We wait for the bus at Port Authority Terminal, and while Marty is in the men's room we discuss plans for how we can get him and his virginity to part company. Marty is eighteen, and it is decided that the time has come. He is the last one remaining in our group who has had but two sexual partners: his right hand and his left hand. For variety, he likes to switch off, so he won't tire of either. He's even named them, "Lefty Lucy" and "Righty Rita."

When he returns from the john we tell him that we are working on some ideas that will get him laid. He says he is perfectly content with his sex life as it currently stands—so to speak.

"Don't worry," I assure him. "By the end of the weekend, you will no longer be a virgin, even if I have to fuck you myself."

Marty grimaces at the thought.

"Just kidding," I assure him several times.

"This not a funny subject, for me, you know, Hank."

Remembering an earlier incident with his former scoutmaster, I quickly move on to another subject.

The waiting area fills quickly. It will be a full busload. Two girls arrive together. They are sixteen or seventeen. They seem shy. One of them has red hair and coke bottle glasses. The other is cute and a little pudgy.

"Hi, my name's Hank," I say.

"I'm Sarah and she's Priscilla," says Miss Cute and Pudgy.

"That's Marty, Billy and Teddy."

They wave.

"We're all going up to Marlborough in the Poconos, what about you girls?"

"Yeah?" said Sarah. "Us too!" She had a *Jersey City-ese* accent you could cut with a chain saw.

"Wait, who's the tall one?" asks Priscilla, in a voice reminiscent of fingernails on a blackboard.

"You mean the one with his fly open? That's Marty."

They both look away, blushing. Marty makes the necessary adjustment to his zipper.

"Thanks, you ffffuck," Marty hisses at me.

"You're welcome."

"Why do you have to embarrass me like that?" he whispers, red faced.

"What are you worried about? She likes you, and she probably appreciates the fact that you're ready for action."

"Funny," he says.

The announcement is made to board, and we drag our gear around to the side of the bus to load it.

"Careful with that." I tell the porter, pointing to the valise holding Frank's disassembled body.

"Sure thing," he mutters, accompanied by a look that fails to instill confidence, and then hurls the suitcase into the luggage compartment.

As we board, I position myself between Sarah and Priscilla, forcing them apart. Before Sarah can complain, she is sitting in the window seat, as I occupy the one next to it. Priscilla appears confused and sits down directly behind us. Passengers fill the bus in a steady stream. The only unoccupied seat is the one next to Priscilla, and the only remaining standee is Marty. The Lord works in mysterious ways, I think.

I overhear Marty talking to Priscilla, boasting of his Sinatra collection. I glance back and observe that Priscilla hangs on every word spoken by Marty, as if she is in the company of genius. Teddy and Billy sit in the seats in front of us. Teddy turns around from time to time, in most cases with his notorious snot rag close to his face.

Teddy is constantly conflating his pickup lines so that they become totally nonsensical. "So, where have you been all my life, before, baby?" he asks Sarah.

She responds with "Hah?" *Jersey City-ese* for "Huh?"

Teddy mutters something indistinguishable, for which I am grateful. He then turns to face front, for which I am equally grateful. I can now practice my charm on this succulent young thing next to me. She is warm and has a hearty laugh. Did I mention cute? Certain of my body parts are beginning to fall deeply in love with her.

"Do you ride?" I ask her.

"I never tried it," she responds, "but I'm willin' to loin."

"Careful how you say 'loin'. It gets me very excited," I say. She responds with a giggle.

The trip is filled with poignant moments like these.

It is three thirty p.m. as our bus pulls into town, dropping us off at a *White Castle* where we're told the ranch will send a jitney to pick us up. We buy bags of sliders, even though the ranch includes meals in the room price. Besides, dinner won't be served for at least two hours. We ravenously consume the contents of what seems an endless bag of a barely identifiable beef product. Just as we complete this sumptuous repast, an old *Woodie* rolls up.

The words "MARLBOROUGH Dude Ranch" can be deciphered through a thick encrustation of mud. Its driver is a very tall cat in a ten-gallon, and a western shirt. He rises out of the old station wagon in what seems to take minutes until all of him is finally out of the vehicle. We stare up in awe of his towering height, including Billy, who is, himself, six foot 1.

"Anyone here for Marbura?" he shouts.

Hands shoot up in affirmation amid cheers and a few whistles.

"Well, hop in, then. Name's Don—Don Malibrand. I'm social director of Marbura. Don't worry about your stuff. My brother, Luke, in the pickup over there, will get your bags. If you all can't fit in the *Wood*ie you can ride with Luke."

Luke acknowledges us with a finger touching the brim on his western hat. His lean face is expressionless and a stalk of grass protrudes from his thick lips. It bobs up and down in a cadence produced by his chewing of either gum or tobacco. Both brothers share the 'tall and thin' gene.

It is obvious that all passengers will not fit in the station wagon—a nine-seater. We scramble for the *Woodie* to avoid being stuck riding outside with the luggage, or worse, inside with Luke. Teddy actually prefers the pickup, feeling a common bond that may trace its ancestry to a more primal period. No one tries to talk him out of it.

Somehow, I manage, once again, to separate Miss Cute 'n Pudgy from Miss Coke Bottles. Sarah is convinced, with some persuasion from me, that she will be more comfortable atop my lap. No garment's thickness can prevent glands from doing what they do best. The ride over poorly paved road provides the rest. Donald takes every mountain curve with the adroitness of an *Indy 500* driver, and with equal speed. The sway and roll of the vehicle keeps John Thomas and me at the peak of excitement. The look on Sarah's face indicates that she is either coming or going. I can't quite decide which.

We begin the curve downward of a rather steep grade. Our driver turns his head toward us to point out places of interest along the narrow road to which he appears to pay no attention. It seems an eternity since Donald has glanced forward through his windshield. He makes eye contact with me and reminds me what beautiful country this is, while simultaneously making adjustments to the position of the steering wheel. As he speaks, a cigarette filter is tightly clutched between his very many white teeth. I can actually hear several passengers praying.

Just as we round a hairpin turn at about fifty-five, Luke's pickup passes us, honking as it flies by, missing a sideswipe by about a coat of paint. Teddy leans through the window so that his entire upper torso protrudes out, his arms flailing wildly in the air, shrieking "Yeeeh-hah", as they whiz past.

"Oh, so that fucker wants to play," says Donald. "This will call for some serious driving…"

The *Woodie* catches up to the pickup attempting to pass. Now multiple "Yeeh-hahs" can be heard from the two Malibrands and a Finkle. At this point I close my eyes and wonder if there really is a God, and if so, did He really create the Malibrands in His image?

I no longer feel the jet-propelled motion of the vehicle. Yet to open my eyes, I conclude that we have either arrived at our destination, or that I am dead. Voices and heavy sighs of relief indicate the former. Finkle approaches our vehicle. His familiar shit-eating grin is displayed as a badge of courage.

"Huh, huh, huh," he chortles. "You should have seen the look on your face. I thought you were ready to shit in your pants," he taunts.

"I think one of us did," I say, alluding to Marty's accident, just now becoming aware of it, as he walks briskly toward the latrine with something very heavy in the back of his brand new *Wranglers*. A chorus of boy laughter rings out.

I kiss Sarah good-bye and tell her to keep an eye out for us in the mess hall.

"Whadaya gawna wear, tonight?" she asks.

"Sorry," I reply. "I am sworn to secrecy."

"Oh pleeeze," she begs.

"What's it worth to you?" I ask with a devilish smile.

"You're disgusting. Don't boys think about anything else?"

"You mean there is something else?"

Chapter 26 • Eyes on the Prize

"You must never be satisfied with losing. You must get angry, terribly angry, about losing. But the mark of the good loser is that he takes his anger out on himself and not his victorious opponents or on his teammates."

-Richard M. Nixon

We check in and are assigned one cabin for the four of us. Marty and I take bottom bunks and Teddy and Billy are okay with toppers.

Marty announces his feeling of relief after his shower, as do the rest of us for his having taken one. There isn't much time to lose. We must unpack and reassemble Frank, plug him in and make sure he works. We will also have to get our costumes ready so that we can change into them after dinner. I remind myself that I have not yet devised a plan to bring Marty into the 'initiated' world.

As we unpack we decide on a nickname for Priscilla. It is unanimously concluded that she is thin enough that in the dark she could be confused with a telephone pole. Billy comes up with the name "Spare-rib." We knew we had asked Billy to join us on this trip for a reason.

Dinner is served camp style, where all line up and plates are filled with a gloppy substance. I turn my eyes away as the unidentifiable matter is dumped on my metal plate. Luke is the one plopping. I have yet to hear him speak. There is a spittoon on the floor directly behind Luke. I am hoping he doesn't get confused, as if anyone could tell.

We are seated on hard wooden benches at wide tables. The ranch house cafeteria is bustling with dudes and dudesses, some of whom are already in costume. I see nothing that I consider a serious challenge to what we have planned.

Sarah and the Spare-rib enter the room dressed as cowgirls. "How original," I think.

They are on the chow line. I can't help notice the look on Luke's lanky face as they step up to his crucible. His expression indicates that had he gone to school, he would have achieved a Doctorate in Lechery.

"Will you girls be need'n anything else?" he asks.

"It talks," I say.

"I don't tink so," says Sarah.

"Nah," echoes the Spare-rib. "We don't tink so."

Luke, registering disappointment, drops very small portions on each of their plates.

"I guess he showed them," I observe.

They arrive at our table. We spread out allowing them room to sit. The Spare-rib is unable to take her eyes off Marty's face as she sits down next to him. Not realizing the lopsided angle of her tray she manages to spill most of her Kool-Aid right onto his crotch. It matches the other food stains on his clothing so he barely notices.

"Well you could at least offer to wipe it off," I suggest. The Spare-rib turns beet red.

"Hank!" admonishes Sarah.

"Nice costumes," I say. "How'd you get the idea?" I try to do this with a straight face, but it is impossible because Teddy is laughing hysterically. His laugh is hard to duplicate. I believe only certain wounded jungle animals are capable of it.

"How come you're not in costume?" asks Sarah.

"We have very special outfits which we're saving for the contest," I explain.

"What contest?" she asks.

"Yeah. What contest?" echoes the Spare-rib.

"You mean you don't know about the competition to win a free weekend?" I query, pointing to the banner high up on the rafters announcing, "Marlborough Annual Halloween Masquerade—Prizes Awarded for the Best Costumes—First Prize: a Free Weekend Stay At Marlborough."

"Gee, we didn't know," say Sarah and Priscilla simultaneously. "It's a good thing we got these!"

"Right," I agree, "especially since the prizes will be based on originality."

The liveliness of our conversation is interrupted by the stick-figure of Don Malibrand standing before, and tapping on the microphone. The pole on the mike stand is almost of sufficient girth to entirely obscure him from view.

"Can I have your attention, ladies and gentlemen?" bellows from the P.A. system, accompanied by feedback loud enough to cause hearing loss in a cadaver. He pounds the mic several times, which sounds like a cannonade. People react by covering their ears with both hands.

"That a little loud?" he asks. "Luke, can you turn that down a mite? We don't wanna make these people deaf."

It's nice to see these Malibrands showing such concern for the safety and well-being of their guests, a kindness not clearly demonstrated by the trip from the depot.

"As many of you know, we will be giving away a free weekend for the best costumes presented before the judges, tonight. We will introduce the judges at eight thirty p.m., just before the contest begins.

"Now I see some mighty swell costumes out there already, and I'm hopin' that those not in costume now, will be by the start of the event. Make sure you register with Gladys, if you haven't already done so. She's my sister, by the way. Gladys'll be around to hand out the contest registration cards—only to registered guests of Marbura. So if you ain't registered, you don't belong here no how, no way. Ain't that right, Gladys?"

"Yup", comes a reply from directly behind our table. It matches the timbre of its masculine counterpart, and this is without the microphone. I turn to put a face on the voice. Gladys has inherited many of the Malibrand features, but slenderness is not one of them. She seems to have inherited the dimensions gene from the livestock on the property.

At this point I am grateful that Teddy took my advice and paid for his room.

Gladys catches me looking at her and there is a sparkle in her eye. "I got yours right here, honey," she beams.

I glance toward heaven, this time praying to the mythical Gods that she is referring to the registration card.

"Now you just fill that in real good," she says, "and if you need help, ole Gladys is here to assist you in anythang you need."

"I…I'll keep that in mind," I reply, amazed that these people are actually from Pennsylvania. Now I know why she didn't accompany her two siblings to the depot. She was busy hauling hog feed, after the tractor broke down.

The registration card is printed on stationery featuring the *Malibrand Manure Farms* logo. Their slogan, "If It's Malibrand Manure—Your Sure—It's Pure," adorns the card in a tasteful Old English typeface. Had I been their marketeer, I would have used the line: "Malibrand Manure—We Have our Shit Together."

The card requires your name, address and phone, along with the character your costume seeks to portray. I figure, if you have to say who (or what) you are, your costume is not very good. Gladys stands over me as I fill out my card, blocking almost all the light. I am about to suggest that she move over a room, but quickly come to my senses. I pretend not to notice her, as if one could fail to be aware of a large pack animal in one's living room.

We return the completed registration cards to Gladys, who pulls them out of my grasp, being careful to brush her baseball-mitt-sized hands against mine. A wave of nausea and fear ripples through my stomach and lodges in my throat.

Don Malibrand announces, "The number on your card is the order that your costume is viewed by the judges—so remember your number. You will be called by your number. No exceptions will be made."

We look at one another and shrug, in a unanimous gesture. No one of us kept the number. I have to chase Gladys down and get the numbers off the cards. She is not difficult to spot, despite the commissary being full to capacity.

"Hey, Gladys," I call.

"Hay is for horses, Sugar," she replies as we make eye contact.

I ignore a temptation and ask her if I can see our cards and get the numbers.

"Well, I don't know sweetie, how bad do you wannum?" she bellows, then followed by a lusty laugh.

I manage a sickly smile as I am handed cards to pore through. Gladys' corpulent frame presses against me as I search through several dozen cards.

"Can't let those outta my sight, Sugar," she says.

Ours are the last cards in the stack. I write on all our cards that they are to be presented as a group. Our numbers begin with twenty-one. I do an end-run around Gladys to rejoin our table.

People have made trips to the dessert line, as cups of Jell-O now appear on the table. "Is there no luxury held back?" I exclaim in wonderment.

It's eight fifteen. Although our group will not be called for several hours, I like to be prompt. I examine myself in the mirror as I apply the finishing touches to my makeup. With my hair parted down the middle, and white powder over my face, I make an acceptable Zacherle, a clown who does a ghoulish local TV show in New York. The real Zacherle shows classic horror movies on Friday and Saturday night interrupted constantly by real and gag commercials, and references to a wife who is supposedly contained in a sarcophagus on camera. Although the wife is never seen, very strange noises are emitted from the cement box, from which he constantly removes things that might be preventing her from resting in peace. These include strings of delicatessen meats, as well as a plethora of plumbing equipment, etc. He refers to her only as "My dear." Sometimes he has to perform emergency surgery on her, and he can be seen aiming chain saws, electric drills, and hypodermic syringes of mammoth proportions in her direction. Dynamite sticks are sometimes used to correct a particularly stubborn medical problem.

Teddy is applying black lipstick, as demanded by his role as *Drecula*, the

Jewish Vampire. With borrowed tux and theatrical cape, combined with his Alfred E. Newman face, he resembles what would be the offspring of a marriage between the *Wicked Witch of the North* and *Howdy Doody*. Bela Lugosi need not look for work, just yet.

Marty makes an impressive Igor. He can contort his face as if it were rubber, placing the left side of his left lower lip somewhere below his chin. With the aid of theatrical makeup, he is able to appear as if he has only one ear.

Shy Billy elects not to don a costume. He has, however, consented to assist us with the abundance of props we will use in tonight's event.

We are all dressed and ready to descend upon the *Ranch House Playhouse*, as it so cleverly called. Frank is resplendent in his finery, and his voice has been thoroughly tested. He must be shielded from prying eyes and a sheet is draped over him to guarantee his anonymity. We carry him to the hall where he will lay undercover until his moment arrives.

The judges are introduced, and to everyone's surprise, they are none other than the Malibrands. They sit at the far end of the stage at a long table upon which sits a microphone, pads of paper and cardboard placards with large numbers emblazoned upon them.

We sit through a seemingly endless parade of contestants, all of whom think that they will win the free weekend. The fact that everyone who has come up in anything remotely resembling a costume has received at least an 8.0 rating from these very discerning judges. One guy masquerades as a civilian and gets an 8.2.

Contestant number twenty is called. We all taste bile in the knowledge that we will be next. The contestant is dressed as a box of Ex-Lax. His name is Elmer and he is one of the locals. He makes a convincing laxative, and we worry as Don reveals a 10. The crowd goes crazy. Luke sneaks a peek at his brother's rating and fishes through his pile for a 10 of his own. As he reveals it, another deafening roar is heard from the excited crowd. Luckily for us, Gladys is more discriminating and gives Mr. Ex-Lax a 7. This brings Elmer's score to a 9.0, making him the winner so far. Don casts Gladys a dirty look, but she pays no attention, beaming a giant smile, revealing teeth reminiscent of a white Baby Grand.

Don goes over his list and announces the score. "Well, this is how we stand so far: In third place, contestant number four, Birdie Kichowski, of Homer Pennsylvania. That's so close right down the road you can spit on it—and huh, huh, huh, most of us do, huh, huh, huh."

Luke appreciates this homeboy humor and chuckles in unison. "Birdie was dressed as a giant turkey, and won a score of 8.6. Mack Maxon, known around these parts as 'Fred Pennsylvania', got himself an 8.8 for his very original walking outhouse costume.

"And, a course, our last contestant, Elmer Germermeir, with a 9.0 that shoulda been at least a 9.7, but the judges have ruled.

"There will be a ten minute intermission before we call our next contestants."

This throws off my stride. I am not expecting an intermission. I will have to psyche myself up again, and inspire my troops as well. But this respite gives me an opportunity to accomplish the other task that lies before me: To be able to count Marty among the non-virgins. I whisper to the Sparerib that I need to discuss something important with her—in private.

"What is it?" she asks.

"Not here. I must discuss something confidential with you about our friend Marty."

We slip out of the playhouse and into the night air.

"What is this all about?"

"You have to promise not to tell a soul, not even Sarah."

"Well, I don't know. Sarah's my best friend. We tell each other everything."

"All right, forget it," I say.

"No, tell me. I promise I won't mention it to Sarah."

"How do you feel about Marty?" I ask.

"I like him. I think he's really cute."

"Well, he likes you too, but he has never been able to make it with a female."

"Whaddaya mean make it?"

"You know, he never gets aroused by girls, and we're worried about him. We think he may be…"

"A homo?" she shrieks.

"Shhh—not so loud. We don't really think he is; it's just that he never meets anyone sexy enough to get him, you know, excited."

"What makes you think I could get him excited?"

"Just look at you in that cowgirl dress. If anyone could get him turned on, it's you. The one thing he doesn't need is to be rejected by a cute girl like you. That could be just the thing to set him on the wrong path. I'm sure you wouldn't want that on your conscience."

"No, I wouldn't," she confirms.

"Just think of what an important role you'll be playing in his development."

"I'll do it," she states with a grin that almost exceeds the width of her scrawny face.

"Remember," I say, my forefinger perpendicular to my lips. "Not a word to anyone."

She nods and we return to the playhouse.

As we enter, Don Malibrand is at the microphone, announcing our numbers. "This next contestant is actually three contestants—presented as a single entry. Are numbers twenty-one through twenty-three here?"

"Yes sir," I shout, as we unveil our life-sized doll and walk him up to the stage. Billy and Marty place a table up onto the stage, while Teddy plugs in the *Webcor* and makes final connections to Frank's internal wiring system. The monster is carefully laid down on the table.

"This here's number twenty-one, twenty-two and twenty-three, Teddy Finkle as Dracula…"

"That's *Drecula*," Teddy corrects.

"Hank Katz as Zacherle, and Marty Rose as Eyegore. These boys are all from Brooklyn, but I don't know who this dead looking one is. I hope it's not something he ate in the mess hall—huh, huh, huh, huh."

Teddy leans over the monster, his cape pulled over the lower part of his face.

"Ah, just what we need: Fresh blood," says Teddy in his best Transylvanian accent, revealing a gruesome set of vampire teeth. He holds up a beaker of red liquid that appears to emerge from the monster's chest.

"Oh, have a heart," says Marty. "He's been through such an ordeal."

"I think I will," I say, pretending to pull a blood soaked organ from Frank's coat.

Then Frank gets into the act as his speaker system comes alive with Billy working the tape recorder. There are occasional bursts of laughter from this very sophisticated audience. A tapping on the microphone from the judges' bench is quickly followed by Don speaking.

"All right, we got to move awn. The judges will now vote."

He pulls up a 7, as does Luke, at first holding it upside down. Even Gladys's 10 is not enough to save the day for us, and we forlornly exit the stage, dragging our equipment with us. It never occurred to me that the Malibrands would have no idea who our characters were.

Several of us decide to stick around in hopes that the judges will miraculously come to their senses and reverse their decisions. We are also hoping for world peace, immortality and way better prizes in *Cracker Jack* boxes.

Not all of us remain in the playhouse. As I scan the premises I notice the absence of both Marty and the Spare-rib.

So it shouldn't be a total loss, I walk Sarah back to her bunkhouse. She knocks gently on the door and gratefully receives no reply. We enter and spend the next two hours in her bed. Life is good. When my energy runs out, I excuse myself, and head back to my room. A scrawny, disheveled, yet beaming, redhead passes me in the autumnal night

I enter the ranch house and turn on a light. Marty is in a deep sleep in his bunk. On his countenance, is the look of a contented child. A peaceful smile adorns a face that still has traces of Igor, AKA *Eyegore*, makeup.

The next morning, over pancakes and sausages, we heap congratulations on Marty and lament about the contest.

None of us can believe that we didn't beat the Ex-Lax, let alone the walking outhouse.

Chapter 27 • Borscht Belt vs. Bible Belt

"Eighty percent of married men cheat in America. The rest cheat in Europe."

-Jackie Mason

Summer—my favorite time of the year—is finally here. College is not quite as bad as high school, but when one is forced to spend time cooped up in a classroom for several hours a day, one does daydream of other possibilities.

It's Wednesday, July 1. We've got my '56 *Karmann Ghia* ready to deliver Marty and me to our summer gig at Grossinger's, the *Queen of the Catskill Resorts*. The car is yellow with a beaten up gray top to match the rest of its condition. There isn't a whole lot of room for a driver and a passenger and enough luggage and toys for a summer away. But we jam it all in, leave the top down and hope it doesn't rain.

Some of our buddies have already left for their jobs in the Catskills. This is summer work—not a career, but with perks such as free eats and the use of some of the fancy hotel facilities, what could be bad? By free food, we were told that meals prepared for guests that remained unserved would be ours for the taking. They don't call it *Disneyland with knishes* for nothing. We are sure to have a great time stuffing our faces and messing with guests' young daughters, not necessarily in that order.

I do enjoy swimming, but according to the "welcome" letter, we are encouraged to use the olympic-sized pool only between the hours of six and seven in the morning. Maybe I don't enjoy swimming quite that much?

Marty is excited, not just for those hot females, but because he expects to see some of his favorite singers, like Eddie Fisher, and comedians like Myron Cohen performing in the region throughout the summer. There'll be celebrities like Milton Berle—on a stage and not just on a tiny screen. Henny Youngman, Buddy Hacket, Don Rickles and one of my personal favorites—Sid Caesar—will be making the scene. They are what *Borscht Belt humor* is all about. Oh, did I forget to mention Jack E. Leonard? He's the man who makes an art out of being obnoxious.

Finkle was here last year. He told us about Micky Katz's (no relation to my family) rendition of *Duvid Crocket—King of Delancey Street*, and how he cracked up laughing. Of course we all knew it didn't take much to crack up Teddy Finkle.

It wasn't a tough decision. We might have taken summer jobs in Kansas or Utah, but as belts go, *Borscht* always wins out over *Bible*. You won't find too many Jewish comedians in those other places.

We're looking at a two hour drive to Sullivan County from our starting point. That's if I drive. If it's Marty behind the wheel you can double that time. He could have learned to drive from my father, whose speedometer complains if it exceeds fifty mph.

The weather is perfect. We're confident we'll make it to our destination with no threat of rain. This is good for us—and our belongings, piled haphazardly in the back of the convertible.

We plan a lunch stop at the Red Apple Rest—mandatory for any trip to the *Jewish Alps*. They have the best burgers and fries along Route 17. But I'm always a little reluctant when the two of us sit down in a restaurant. Marty can sometimes be an embarrassment at a dinner table. For example, he hasn't yet learned how to politely excuse himself to go to the gentlemen's room. Instead he announces in graphic detail exactly which bodily function he is about to perform. "Too much information," I tell him, but does he get it? If that should happen again I'm prepared to pretend that I don't know him.

Marty has an insatiable appetite. And it's only the inevitable intestinal cramps that let him know when it's time to stop inhaling his food. After getting into the car to resume our trip I hear incessant complaints about his stomach, usually followed by loud explosions from his rear. Fortunately we are riding in an open car; this helps, but only somewhat.

We are to start working first thing tomorrow, and report to the kitchen at six a.m., a truly ungodly hour. But we will arrive at Grossinger's in less than an hour, giving us a chance to look around, get familiar with the place and maybe meet some chicks.

We arrive at what looks to us like a very impressive building front. There are several young men standing outside ready to perform valet service for the hotel's customers. In their regal attire, they look more like they're on duty at Buckingham Palace. When they get a look at our beat up VW, they don't confuse us with hotel guests. They direct us to a parking area the equivalent of several blocks away, keeping the immediate area for valet and guest parking.

We're told where new employees are to check in and make our way to a shack with a hand-painted sign reading "Kitchen Help." No expense was spared in making this cabin a welcoming place for Grossinger's culinary staff. Just trudging through a jungle of weeds to get to the door is a challenge.

We knock on a decrepit old door with its torn screen for several minutes. Having gotten no response, we finally push it open. Inside, seated at a beat-up desk is the welcoming committee of one. He chews on what remains of a lit cigar without bothering to look up.

"Excuse me," I call to him. Now his stubbly face can be seen in its full glory.

"Yeah," it answers.

"We're here for kitchen crew duties. We're supposed to start tomorrow morning. Are you Jeb?"

"That's what they call me," he says.

"I'm Hank Katz."

"And I'm Marty Rose. I think we are supposed to have orientation. Are you the guy that does that?"

"Yeah, give me a minute and we'll go over to the dorms. Later I'll introduce you and show youze around."

His rotund body rises slowly from his seat. Visible from the top of his pants is a generous swatch of polka dotted undershorts peeking out over his belt. Very flattering. He spends a few moments in a vain attempt to make himself presentable.

"Youze guys are the first to arrive. We officially open for the season tomorrow morning."

He escorts us to a dilapidated building in which a very large staff will be sleeping. The structure could win an award in the delayed maintenance category.

"Okay, this here's the dorm. Since you're the first ones here, you get your pick of the best bunks."

It's hard to come up with the adjectives to describe the beauty of this room, but underwhelming comes to mind. Out of the dozens available, Marty and I choose a single bunk with me on the top and him down below. After poking a multitude of mattresses to try to find one that wasn't used as part of a torture device during the Spanish Inquisition, we finally select one that is moderately acceptable. Well, at least it's near a window.

The shower and sanitary facilities—if they could be called that—are outdoors, naturally.

Jeb tells us we should get the stuff out of our car and haul it back here. He plans to wait until more troops arrive so that he doesn't have to give the kitchen orientation any more than necessary.

Our stomachs tell us it must be getting close to the dinner hour, though we really have no idea when that will be. Another reason for gastric restlessness might be attributed to the fact that neither of us has ever worked in a kitchen—let alone a large resort restaurant. Marty is particularly nervous because he has a propensity to drop things. If one of those objects happens to be a tray, and the target is the lap of resort guest—the outcome might not be so pleasant.

The closest I've ever gotten to serving food is opening a can of *Chef Boyardee* and dumping it into a pot for my sister. But I'm a charmer. I will earn big tips as a waiter because I know how to bullshit. I'm also good at remembering what people tell me, and I will use that skill to take guest's orders without even writing them down. That should wow 'em.

We sit around this large table amidst the other staff that steadily meander in. Out of a kitchen crew of fifty-four, thirteen are girls around our age; twelve are much older women. The rest are males ranging in age from eighteen to about sixty. The half-eaten meal before us is not the fare we can expect once guests arrive. This one fits more the description of what might be served at a soup kitchen.

Marty is on my right and Angela, a plain looking girl in her late teens who hails from Woodstock, not very far from here, is to my left. Her very short skirt is hiked up about as far as the legal limit would permit. Her cheap perfume is having a negative effect on my appreciation of dinner— not that it would take much. I finally realize why it's called "toilet water."

Marty, having caught a glimpse of a healthy pair of thighs, whispers in my ear, "Do you think we could change seats so I can get a little closer to Angela? She's *zaftig*—just the way I like them."

I am pleased to observe that Marty seeks to broaden his pleasure horizons, that have thus far been mostly limited to self-gratification.

"Sure," I say, always happy to oblige, and to also put a little distance between me and her *Eau de Terrible*.

"Dessert is now available," comes the announcement over the loudspeakers. My hopes are dimmed, as J-e-l-l-o now appears on the counter, ready to be devoured by this gastronomically erudite crowd. I now feel as though I never left home.

Jeb had warned us that the playing of *Reveille* would awaken us. When it comes, before the sun has risen, it is not particularly appreciated. I assume that the hotel's guests will not be awakened in the same way—or at the same time. After a group yawn we all dress and make our way to the kitchen. All of us allegedly know what to do, having gone through Jeb's orientation the afternoon before.

No guests have yet arrived, giving us time to grab some coffee. Marty has a little with his cup of milk and sugar. I have weaned myself away from those accoutrements, knowing that if the alleged Supreme Being had wanted coffee to be consumed that way he would have grown the coffee tree thusly.

Now that I've consumed five cups of java waiting for the room to fill with guests and get on with the job I was hired to do, I'm a little caffeine shaky. I look up to discover an entourage of eight people moving toward one of my assigned tables. It's an odd configuration consisting of a single older man with seven young ladies of college age.

After they are seated I nervously approach them and introduce myself. "Good morning," I say, the caffeine rendering that greeting into one syllable.

"I'm Hank, and I'll be your server. Please let me know if there's anything you need."

"Some coffee would be lovely," says the gentleman, in a crisp British accent. "And ladies, tell the young man what you want to drink."

"Hank, please calm down. We're not going to bite you, unless, of course, we're not fully satiated by the Grossinger's breakfast."

"That's funny, Professor Kornbluth," says one comely young member of the group. "I'll have some cocoa, please."

The others each order a beverage. "And menus would be extremely helpful," the professor chimes in.

I hand out eight menus, after having clumsily dropped two on the floor. "Sorry. No more coffee for me for the rest of the summer," I blurt out.

After giving them a chance to review the menu I inform them that they can either order from it, or serve themselves from the generous breakfast buffet, naturally hoping that they'll choose the latter.

They all get up to peruse the long buffet table, with the exception of a sweet young thing who tells me her name is Phyllis. I soon learn about the gentleman of the party, who happens to be Dr. Nigel Kornbluth, a visiting professor from Oxford University. He'll be leading a two-week seminar on King Richard III, that NYU is sponsoring right here at Grossinger's.

"European History. That happens to be my major. I'm nuts about the subject," I say with some renewed confidence.

"I'm looking forward to working with Professor Kornbluth, " says Phyllis, "He's dreamy."

I conclude that we have different definitions for "dreamy."

My guests, having finished their breakfast, will now head for the classroom where Dr. Kornbluth will do his thing. I would have done anything to attend, but that is not what Grossinger's hired me for. He will teach these eager to learn young ladies, including the dreamer, about the most reviled king in all of British history. Having read quite a bit on the subject I was hoping for a chance to at least discuss the last Plantagenet king with the professor.

Marty and I got through a full day of waitering and bussing. No major accidents to report, we are grateful to observe. Phyllis mentioned earlier that her gang was getting together this evening for a little welcome party for the professor. My duties will be over for the day, and I'll be free to find some form of entertainment.

Marty is about to leave with fellow kitchen staff to test his skills at bowling. The word "skills" here may be a stretch. I've seen Marty bowl. I've also observed his telling off-color jokes. I wasn't sure which spent more time in the gutter, his mind or his ball. I opt out of joining them with the hopes that my appearance at Kornbluth's party will be welcomed.

I head to the room where Phyllis told me the party was being held. Apparently, the professor threw a few shillings to the check-in clerk, giving his group access to room 418, which was unrented. The celebration should be well on its way. I exit the elevator and can't fail to smell the ganja pervading the hallway. It gets more pungent as I approach the door. I've never smoked pot, but have been around it enough to know what it is. There is loud music playing; it stops when I knock.

Professor Kornbluth opens the door a crack to see who the intruder might be. "Oh, it's Hank, the waiter with the photographic memory. Please do come in."

Honored to have received this invitation, I slip into the room, and the music resumes. Some of the girls seem glad to see me. The professor's eyes bear the glassy look of one who's indulged in the smoking of the pernicious weed. Most others are in a similar state.

I'm invited to share in the enjoyment of this intoxicant. I previously believed all the hype, warning that its use could lead to addiction, and that it was an inevitable pathway to much stronger drugs. But seeing the contented look on practically everyone's face, plus the knowledge that if I stayed in this smoke-filled room, I'd get high, whether or not I actually partook.

At first it seems that the drug has absolutely no affect on me. However, I do feel a rapacious hunger, despite having had more than a normal serving of dinner—not to mention two blueberry cheesecake desserts. Between moments of stuffing my face with the snacks that are ubiquitous throughout this room, I attempt to converse with the guest of honor. He is more than appropriately close to one of the girls. Having his hand on a young girl's thigh seems like a new way for the professor to teach English history.

"So what about the princes?" I ask him. "Did he kill them or not?"

"If you're referring to Edward and Richard, potential heirs of Edward IV, and whether Richard of York struck the mortal blows, I think it's something we shan't ever know." The effects of the marijuana don't seem to have crippled his ability to articulate.

"Doesn't most of Richard III's derision come from Shakespeare?" I ask.

Kornbluth is about to reply, but is halted by a very unwelcomed pounding on the door. This is followed by the shouts of "Police—open up!"

This room does adjoin another. There was a plan in place for just such an emergency, to vacate by using the common door to exit, and escape through the other room's door. I was not privy to this cunning arrangement. The folks banging on the door do not seem like they would appreciate waiting. As I open it, I'm bowled over as several burly men in western hats barge through, weapons drawn. From my new position, sprawled on the floor, I notice that I am the only guest remaining.

I almost managed a full twenty-four hours at Grossinger's without getting into deep shit.

Chapter 28 • Graduation Day

"The fireworks begin today. Each diploma is a lighted match. Each one of you is a fuse."

-Ed Koch

I thought I'd never live to see it. In fact, based on my less than stellar high school record, I didn't think I would ever see the inside of a college campus, let alone graduate from one. But I bore down in my last year at *Erasmus Hall*, the high school I switched to after being taken away in handcuffs from *SIA*. With sacrificial hours of summer school, help from a sympathetic guidance counselor, combined with expert cheating techniques, I had somehow managed to make my parents proud.

Wearing the familiar cap and gown, I make my way to the *CUNY* auditorium. That annoying tassel keeps swinging back in forth, marring my vision, as I hasten my step so I won't be late for the ceremony. This is not a day to oversleep, and I probably should have forestalled the celebratory party until the night after the graduation. I am never one to subscribe to the delayed gratification theory. The very thought that I am no longer condemned to walk these hallowed halls again, cries out the word PARTY!

And a hell of a shindig it was. Gopher, who had graduated two weeks earlier (from Harvard, no less), planned the whole thing, arranging for copious quantities of alcoholic and herbal substances, and female acquaintances not known for shyness. It began at the late hour of eleven thirty p.m., and that should have told me that it would not end early, unless you regard seven a.m. as early.

There must have been a hundred boisterously drunk and stoned individuals in what was little more than a large studio apartment. You couldn't move an inch without colliding with another similarly blitzed individual. And depending on the collideee, this isn't always an unpleasant experience.

Marty Rose has just returned from military service. In exchange for his two-year sacrifice for his country, he was put in charge of music. After all, he did serve in a battle zone known as Baden-Baden, Germany, albeit twenty-six years after the conclusion of WW2. His selection as DJ might be a mistake. Marty's musical taste ran counter to what the average twenty-one-year-old is expecting. Not a *Louie Louie*, nor a *Surfin' Safari* is to be heard. Instead, we are treated to renditions from Julius LaRosa, Eddie Fisher and a host of other hasbeens of the music world, at least as far as we were concerned. To be fair, he did intersperse his selections with something from Sinatra. Ultimately, I am forced to pull out my record collection, and the party finally comes to life.

He does not take the demotion gracefully, proceeding to imbibe heavily, which, with Marty, is a relative term. He gets sloppy (how unusual), and spills food and beverage on his own, and virtually everyone else's, clothing. No chair, sofa or floor is spared his mouth's constant dripping of effluents. He continues to talk with it full, and he has difficulty keeping his plate at anything close to a ninety-degree angle from the floor.

I find a vacant seat in the fifth row, the last one available. Naturally, I have to make a grand entrance, especially for my graduation. I glance from left to right at the faces of my fellow grads, most of whom I know personally. One is my buddy, Teddy, who, like me, had not been given a strong chance of making it to this august occasion. I recall all of the fine moments we shared, making rockets that failed, and explosives that didn't.

Because of the connections made by his deceased brother, Teddy was guaranteed a good shot at success on Wall Street, despite his lack of a Yale or Harvard degree. I, on the other hand, have no such connections, and am unsure what my career path will be, now that I will be receiving my degree.

"Henry, Henry," I hear a shrill female voice yelling from a distant part of the auditorium. I am annoyed at being awakened until I realize that the voice is trying to tell me to get off my ass and join the procession of fellow graduates who have already lined up to receive their diplomas. The voice belongs to none other than my Mom, who has many hours of practice attempting to wake me from sleep.

My bleary eyes blink as I wipe away the cobwebs and haul my exhausted self out of the chair to join the parade of cheery-eyed young adults. As I wait my turn for a document that will confirm my waste of four long years, I spot my mother and father in the rear of the room. He is resplendent in an outfit he pulled from his closet that would have been fashionable during the Coolidge administration. My teenaged sibling, Sydney, only slightly better dressed, sits to the right of our parents. They all stand and wave. Yes, they are proud of the first of our brood to graduate. My mother is, in fact, *kvelling*. For those not familiar with this *Yiddishism*, it is an expression of pride only a Jewish mother can feel for a child who has graduated from medical or law school, or for a daughter who has married a lawyer or a doctor. So, under those requirements, I am not entitled to the full *kvell*.

Dean Escobar will be calling the names in alphabetical order. With the aid of June, a comely Escobar assistant, I attempt to assimilate into my correct place in the line. I spot Bernie Levy and aim toward his position, thinking, "How far off could I be?" June quietly asks my name, which she checks against the list on her clipboard.

"I'm sorry," she whispers. "I don't seem to have you on my list. Are you sure you've given me the right spelling?"

"I may not be the brightest bulb in the hydroponic hot house, but I think I know how to spell my own name," I hiss back.

"Sorry, there is no Henry Katz on this list. You will have to exit the line."

"What? Get off the line?" comes my indignant reaction, almost drowning out *Pomp and Circumstance* coming from the school band.

I am beet red and about ready to explode when Dean Escobar starts reading the names of those about to receive their diplomas.

"ABBOT, LISA........."

Well, if I can't be found on the list, there is no point remaining in the queue, I think. I angrily pull that dumb looking mortarboard off my head and I'm about to fling it away, and take off, when June finds my name toward the bottom of the list.

"So sorry," she says, with the most embarrassed look. "There must have been a typo. Your name is here, but it's down here with the V's."

Now neither of us knows where I should be in the line, midway or at the tail end. If I stand in the proper spot, and Escobar doesn't have my diploma ready to hand me, it could be awkward. On the other hand, if he does have it, and it's spelled correctly on the diploma, he calls my name and hands the document to the wrong K or possibly to an L.

I unilaterally decide to go to the end of the line in between Sara Vanden Huevel and Michael Zell. June shrugs. This confuses my mom, who has no idea what's going on, but with a surname beginning with the letter 'K' naturally expects me to be somewhere near the middle of the line. I look up at her as she waves her Brownie camera (purchased just for this occasion) in the air in fierce agitation.

After forty-two names are read, and Escobar is well past the L's, I glance toward my parents' seats as they register their disappointment. They shake their heads, looking unhappier than a Goldwater supporter.

I did make the right choice of where to stand. The proof came when Escobar shouted, "VATZ, HENRY".

From all the way up on the stage I can hear my mother in the audience, and she's not exactly swelling with pride.

"Did you hear that, Sol," is my Mom's shocked reaction. "The first Katz to graduate…"

"You mean the first Vatz to graduate," says Dad, attempting to quell her displeasure with a weak attempt at humor.

I accept the parchment from the good Dean without failing to notice the red-faced woman sitting next to the slave-to-fashion man in the penultimate row of the auditorium. I feel bad for my mother, who will be telling this story to her *Mah Jong* buddies, and anyone else she comes across, including the sanitation workers who pick up her trash.

Kvelling is not all that it is cracked up to be.

Chapter 29 • It's Not the School, but the Principal of the Thing

"Always vote for principle, though you may vote alone, and you may cherish the sweetest reflection that your vote is never lost."

-John Quincy Adams

As a kid going to school I dreaded the arrival of the day after Labor Day, that rude interruption of the summer hiatus. But responsible adults should not continue to think this way. That's what I tell myself as I dress for my job interview. My first instinct is to show my mother the outfit I plan to wear, with the intention of looking my best. Who am I kidding? Fashion advice from Edie (or Sol), would be like asking Hitler for 'Being Nice to the Jews' instructions. If I get this job, I may actually be able to afford an apartment of my own. But then I would miss the cooking.

I stare into the bathroom mirror looking for spots that my razor may have missed. Found one. Ouch! Bleeding like a stuck pig. Serves me right for adopting my father's rule about never discarding even very used razor blades. A piece of toilet paper applied to the wound should stop the hemorrhaging. The tissue must be removed from my face before I show up at *Tilden High* for my interview, as it doesn't exactly enhance my appearance.

The position is Substitute History Teacher, an opportunity created because the actual teacher is on maternity leave. I hope to dazzle the principal with my knowledge of the subject, and my charismatic approach to teaching. I won't be making the same mistakes as suffered at the hands of my teachers, who practically bored me to death.

My car is still in the shop. A mature adult would have had its mechanical problems taken care of in a timely manner, and not wait until the last minute. So now I must take public transportation from my parents' apartment to the school—meaning two busses.

I could swear that the bus driver waited for me to arrive at the stop before deliberately leaving me in the wake of his bus fumes. It is rush hour so I'm not expecting a long wait until the next one arrives. Good thing I left the apartment early, which was the accidental result of my alarm clock reading one hour later than the correct time. Fifteen anxious minutes go by.

Finally, one pulls in and I board. No seats, of course. Who am I to complain about having to stand and be tossed around? But does that stop me? I bitch and moan without cessation throughout the ride. People look at me like I'm nuts. They're used to it—New York, not Rio De Janeiro, is the nut capital of the world.

From our position riding up Ralph Avenue, I spot the school around the corner on Tilden Avenue. Same architecture as the grammar school I attended in Crown Heights. It was named for a governor of the state that ran unsuccessfully for the presidency. How do I know this? Why, I'm a history teacher (or hope to be), that's how.

After exiting the bus I look in the side view mirror of a parked car to examine my face for any traces of this morning's razor maiming. No apparent damage. My hair is another story. I can just hear the principal asking me if we have combs where I come from. Since I left mine on the dresser, I spit on my palms and try to smooth down my coiffure as best as I can. There's nothing like being fully prepared for job a interview.

I locate the teachers' entrance and look for signs for the principal's office. I've got three minutes before I'm late. I finally stop a man in a janitor's uniform and get directions in broken English. I'm going to have to hustle to make it on time. I make an assumption that I've heard him correctly. I can hear that voice in my head saying, "Didn't I tell you to leave enough time to arrive for the interview on schedule?"

In my mad dash to reach the Principal's office—naturally it's on the other side of the building—I almost knock over a kid with braces on his legs.

"Hey watch where you're going," can be heard from several voices at once.

I spot the office with the clock over it reading precisely nine a.m. A pretty, young receptionist greets me with the words, "Are you Mr. Katz?"

168

"My father is Mr. Katz. I'm Henry," I respond, my flirt gene in full gear.

"Good morning Mr. Katz. I see that you're right on time for your interview. However, Mr. Birkenstock has not yet arrived. We're expecting him momentarily. In the meantime, please make yourself comfortable over there."

Coffee is offered and it's tempting, but out of fear that I will spill it on myself, I decline. Earlier, I refused a cup of what my mother calls coffee before leaving the apartment. I could say that I miss my mother's coffee—and try to do just that whenever I get a chance. A *New York Times* is offered for my reading pleasure. Why not? Maybe it'll give me something to talk about with my interviewer.

I rifle through the paper trying to find an interesting discussion worthy news story. On page eight there's an article on a Copenhagen man who was attacked by a predator fish while swimming off the *Vista Del Mar*. It seems the poor fellow suffered a loss of his genitalia. "What do you know," I say to no one in particular, "a Danish without nuts."

The receptionist spots me laughing and asks me what I find funny. In a rare moment of sanity I elect not to explain my frivolity. Instead I mention something that was said on *All in the Family* the night before that tickled my funny bone.

I see another article reporting on the refusal of the Kentucky Draft Board to accept Muhammad Ali's appeal for exemption in the military, on the grounds of conscientious objection. If it had been a white guy making a living by punching people in the head, would he have been denied that exemption?

The time on the big clock behind the receptionist reads ten fifteen—so much for on time appointments. Had I known this I wouldn't have rushed my *kishkes*. The *Times* is running out of stories for me to read.

Just then the door opens and in walks Principal Birkenstock. With no apology or even a glance in my direction, he disappears behind his door. The receptionist sends me an understanding shrug.

Another fifteen minutes go by, and after a prompting from me she knocks on his door before entering. Shortly after, she emerges from his office, and with a sympathetic look, tells me that Mr. Berkenstock will see me now.

"Oh, boy!" I exclaim.

The principal sits behind a beat-up oak desk in a chair that has seen better days, motioning for me to sit down. "Good morning, Sir," I say, with no hope that any regrets for his tardiness will be forthcoming.

He grunts back, and I can almost make out the word 'morning' in his reply. He was reading something when I walked in, and continues doing so despite my presence. When he finally deigns to look up he utters, "You're here for what reason?"

He doesn't look old enough for *Alzheimer's*, I think. Can he really not know the purpose of this meeting? "Mr. Birkenstock," I say, "I'm here for the substitute teacher position?" It was more like a question than a reply.

"Which teacher position. We have several open at the moment."

We are now actually having something resembling a dialog. I explained that it is for the history position.

"Do you have your CV?" he mutters.

"Right there on your desk, Mr. Birkenstock. Right there next to your coffee mug. Careful! Whoops! Guess you didn't see the mug," I suggest, after the entire contents of said mug drowns my resume in a sea of brown liquid.

He tries drying off the document with his handkerchief, now also soaked in coffee. "Okay, we'll proceed without the resume. Tell me about yourself."

"Well, Mr. Birkenstock," I reply. "History has been my favorite subject since I was in my junior year of high school." This was partially true, since all I ever learned on the subject was from my own reading—much of which occurred while I was cutting school. "I'm well-schooled in U.S. as well as European, but especially British History."

"Okay," he says. Who was the fifteenth President of the United States?"

"That's too easy. The answer is Buchanan," I reply. "James Buchanan. As a matter of fact I can name all of the U.S. Presidents in order, tell you what state they came from, how many terms they served and the dates of service. I can even tell you…"

"Ok. Stop. I got it. You know the presidents. When were the *Articles of*

Confederation signed?"

This goes on for at least fifteen minutes, and he is unable to stump me even once. I tell him that my teaching methods are not conventional, prompting him to ask me how.

"You see, Mr. B, students don't want to be filled with just the rote information. They need to have their curiosity piqued, coaxing them to want to learn more. For example, George Washington is much more interesting when you know how he dressed, and why he was always misplacing his hat, and what music interested him. Anyone can memorize that the *Battle of Long Island* was fought on August 27, 1776, only a few miles from this very school, by the way, but do we know that his horse had to be replaced at the last minute, due to an injury to his left front hoof? The horse had to be put down, and that put the General in a foul mood. Knowledge like that brings the scene to life."

"Okay, okay. You got the job. Can you start today?"

It's difficult for me to contain my ebullience, naturally I answer in the affirmative. Berkenstock extends a limp hand, which I reach out to grasp. It can only be compared to that of a corpse, but with a much weaker grip.

There is no time for a tour of the building and its facilities as my first class is to begin within minutes. I'm not even sure what the specific history subject will be, having not yet seen a syllabus. But I'm good at faking it, as my own college graduation would attest.

The receptionist, whose name I now know to be "Liz," escorts me to the classroom, with a promise to thoroughly show me around some time later in the day. As she walks in front of me, I'm imagining what her showing me around might be like. I keep hearing that annoying voice warning me to use my brain to think, as opposed to that other organ.

Consulting the sheet of paper upon which all of my courses are listed, I see that this first class is eleventh grade European history. Just before leaving me at the door to the classroom she hands me a textbook and says, "Oh, I think you might need this. And good luck, Mr. Katz."

Memories of my own high school history experience begin haunting me as I enter the empty room. "I am not sixteen years old," I keep repeating.

This is the first day of school. I'm hoping that my students will not share the attitude of my former adolescence as I familiarize myself with the room.

First thing is to try out the chair. Not a bad fit, I think, but a little squeaky. Then I pull each drawer open to examine its contents, including supplies such as pens, pencils and notebooks. There's an attendance sheet in the top drawer. Whoever is in charge of stocking those drawers did a pretty good job, as I seem to have everything I need, except maybe an extra dollop of courage.

With the few minutes remaining before the start of the class, I write my name on the blackboard. It is so illegible that I can barely read it, forcing me to erase it and re-write it several times. Finally, a version not requiring a cryptographer to decipher appears on the board. At last, my name in chalk!

Just as the bell rings, the doors open and my students pour in. I count twenty-seven heads, comparing it to the attendance sheet which says I should be expecting twenty-eight.

"Take your seats please," I shout with a voice that crackles with nervousness.

"My name is Mr. Katz, and I'll be your substitute teacher until Mrs. McInerney returns, if she indeed does. As you may be aware, she is off adding to the already teeming population of Planet Earth." There are but a few smiling faces in appreciation of my remark. "Please consult the blackboard for the correct spelling of my name."

"By the headcount we are short one person, so I will first take attendance. That will also afford me an opportunity to learn your names."

At the conclusion of that ritual I'm ready to begin teaching history the way it is meant to be taught. "Before we begin," I announce, "I'd like to acquaint you with some of the techniques I will employ to make yours a meaningful learning experience. Feel free to raise your hands at anytime if you need me to elucidate."

A hand rises from the rear of the room belonging to Jerome Jefferson, according to the attendance I have just taken. "Yes, Mr. Jefferson, what is your question? And please stand so we can all hear you clearly."

"Mr. Katz, I jess wanna find out just how you are goin' to make the suhject of European History interestin'. I mean, it will take some doin."

"Good observation, Jerome," I answer. "Making the teaching of any subject both informative and fun does take some 'doin', as you put it. But I believe I have discovered ways to make it happen. So, ladies and gentlemen, indulge me.

"Since this is our first class of the school year, let's create a context to learn where many of our ancestors came from. For those of you who don't know what the word 'context' means, I suggest you look it up, as it is an important feature of this methodology.

"According to this textbook, upon which our lessons will be based," I say, holding up the front cover, "we will be covering the history of Europe from the medieval period until the beginning of World War I. Raise your hand if you don't know which years are considered the medieval period."

To my chagrin, almost every hand is raised, with the exception of Jerome's, whose ancestry, I'll wager, does not trace back to European. We shall overcome, I hope, reminded of the civil rights song popularized several years back.

"Ok. I see that I've got some splainin' to do," I say in a weak attempt to sound like Ricky Ricardo. "The medieval period takes in a span of approximately one thousand years, beginning with the year 476 CE, and running through the early sixteenth century. "

Suddenly a dozen hands rise. "You have a question?" I ask. "Let me start with the first hand I saw raised."

A young lady, wearing a cross around her neck, roughly the size of the original crucifix, asks, "What do you mean 'CE'? You said 476 CE. Didn't you mean 'AD'?"

My face becomes flushed because a sensitive subject has been introduced that has hit a nerve. That damn voice is telling me "Don't go there," but do I listen? "Some historians avoid the terms 'AD' and 'BC' because they are biblical references. Not everyone accepts terms that refer to the biblical versions of history. For those of us who like to see evidence before we accept something that has been passed down for generations, using those terms to describe a period is unscientific. So, throughout this course I will be replacing the term 'AD' with the less familiar 'CE', which stands for the Common Era, leaving the Lord out of it completely. Anyone else who had their hand up: do you have a different question?"

And with that, all hands return to their respective desktops. I catch several disenchanted faces among my students. I don't spot the *Star of David* on any of their necks, but the Christian symbol is ubiquitously displayed. So it appears that I may have started a religious war, which, when you think about it, could be fitting for a history course.

We complete an overview of the millennium beginning with the barbaric raids on the Roman Empire, and conclude with the start of the *Renaissance*. Since I have neither studied the material in this textbook nor read the syllabus, I give no homework assignment for tonight. The bell rings and I dismiss the class.

The rest of the day is about the same. A few hostile looks from some in the senior American History class when the 'AD' question arises, but all and all, I'd say the day goes pretty well.

Riding home on the bus I ponder the wisdom of having let my religious beliefs shroud some of the material. "They have a right to know the truth," I say a little too loud, attracting the attention of some fellow passengers.

When I arrive at my apartment I hear the phone ringing as I jiggle the keys to get the door open. It rings several times before I finally reach it to lift the receiver.

"Mr. Katz?" says the voice sounding much like that of Liz, the receptionist. Thinking it was the school calling to congratulate me on a great first day, I say "That you, Liz?"

"Yes it is, Mr. Katz, please hold for Mr. Berkenstock."

Several anxious minutes elapse until the unmistakable, dynamic voice of Mr. B says, "I've heard from several hysterical parents, and I'm afraid I have some bad news."

Chapter 30 • Unveiled

> "In a closed society where everybody's guilty, the only crime is getting caught. In a world of thieves, the only final sin is stupidity."
>
> *-Hunter S. Thompson*

It's been several months since my presence at *Tilden High School* was no longer welcomed. I survive on the little money I earn helping a friend deliver illicit substances to his clients and a little occasional petty thievery. I know I'm taking a chance doing these things. For example, the police do not look kindly on those transporting the evil weed. Why tobacco, which kills millions, is legal, but pot is not, amazes me. But I don't make the drug laws—nor do I obey them.

My last stop today is near Brooklyn's *Pratt Institute*. I simply have to hand off a small envelope in exchange for a wad of bills. The client teaches sculpture at the Institute. He is easy to recognize: very tall, hair that may never have been combed and a straggly beard. The exchange takes place quickly, as we both survey the area for onlookers.

The transaction is for seventy American dollars for a half ounce of Mexican *ganja*. My cut is one third, netting me the enormous sum of twenty-three dollars. But add that to a two ounce envelope I will be dropping off later, and I'm really not having a bad day.

The litter in the streets around here really bugs me. I think it's just as bad as the trash you see on Manhattan streets. Stealing is bad, I know, but for littering? The death penalty!

I wander into the *Casablanca Cafe* on Atlantic Avenue, hankering for a nice Moroccan meal. Nothing like eating with your hands, but taking heed to honor the tradition of never holding food with the left. That is the hand reserved for 'other' functions, and the twain better not meet.

Okay, I confess. There is another reason compelling me to check out this establishment, and it isn't necessarily culinary.

I have walked past this eatery on several occasions, but never before peeked at their menu, nor the large sign posted on the easel just inside their doorway. On it is a poster with a most spectacular looking female, dressed in the costume of an exotic dancer. I certainly heard about belly dancers, but never caught a show. Beneath the photo of the statuesque female the name Zenith Nadir is posted in *Arabesque* lettering.

I have seen that face before, but I can't place it. It will come to me, I'm sure, given my ability to remember everything, at least everything I choose to remember.

I'm greeted by the *Maitre d'*, a very large man dressed like a cast member of *Ali Baba and the Forty Thieves*. He eyes me suspiciously. Apparently my attire fails to impress, and is deemed to be beneath the standard of those patrons already seated. How formally dressed does one need to be in order to sit on the floor to enjoy some *Ferakh Maamer*, soaked up by a serving of *khobz*?

He ushers me to a less prominent location towards the back of the room. Middle Eastern music plays through the sound system, and exotic scents fill the air. I begin to salivate, and want food now. My few surreptitious tokes before entering the restaurant are now heightening my appetite.

Casablanca begins to fill up with, predominantly, couples, who look to be mostly in their forties or fifties. I just may be the youngest patron in the joint.

The show is not starting for a while, so I've got time to peruse the premises, including the coat check lady that I noticed as I walked in. She is cute—but nothing compared to the main attraction, Zenith Nadir. I ask her where the men's room is located.

"The gentlemen's room is down this corridor," she says.

"Gentlemen?" I ask. "Where do you see a gentleman?"

She smiles and tells me that she assumes all men are gentlemen until they prove otherwise.

"Well how do I prove otherwise?"

"Oh, I think you could come up with an idea or two," she says, still smiling.

While we are talking, I'm checking out the coats in the closet just behind her. I wonder just what one might find in the pockets of some of those ritzier outer garments.

As I return from the little boys' room, the sound of what I assume to be belly dancer music can be heard from the main room. How do I know it's belly dancer music? You can just tell.

I return to my seat after telling Miss Hat Check, "See ya later, I hope." That was treated with a shrug, which I took to mean, "Maybe?"

Back at my seat (we can't call it a table), I mop up the remainder of the main dish with the bread and stuff the last vestiges of it into my mouth. With a cup of espresso so thick one needs a knife to separate the grounds, I wait for the main attraction to appear as advertised. I'm still having trouble remembering where I might have met her, when she enters the small wooden stage, with a veil covering her face. This doesn't help with my quest to identify her. I may be the only male in the room looking at the veil, and not certain moving parts. Okay, I admit it. I am looking at certain moving parts, glancing up, only occasionally, to see if her face is exposed.

After fifteen body gyrating minutes the music stops. Miss Nadir pulls off the veil and curtseys before her appreciative audience. It is then that I recognize the face I haven't seen in ten years.

She disappears behind a curtain, and the din of many conversations returns to *Casablanca*.

I skip what looks like a desert that's not made for figure flattering. I leave more than enough cash to cover the check and rise slowly from my uncomfortable, but worth it, sitting position on the floor.

I stop at the hatcheck and ask the attendant, whose name I had earlier neglected to learn, if she knows anything about Zenith.

"Oh, yes," she confirms. "We're actually pretty close friends."

"I believe I know her," I say. "She's someone I met long ago. By the way, my name is Hank."

"Becky," she replies.

"Would you like me to introduce you, or reintroduce you?" she offers.

My eyes light up in the affirmative.

I wait alone outside Becky's domain as she goes to fetch her friend. No one is looking so I stick a hand into the pocket of a man's coat hanging close to door. I feel a small box, and without hesitation, slip it into my pocket, having no idea of its contents. This is not the first time I've done this. We've all got to make a living, I think, defending my actions to no one but myself—and that annoying voice advising me to the contrary.

A minute goes by, and I'm tempted to hightail it out of there without having the pleasure of meeting the exciting Miss Nadir.

They both appear, obviating my desire to scram.

"Hank, meet my friend Zenith Nadir."

"A pleasure," I say. "But I believe we have met before."

"Your face does not ring a bell," says Zenith.

"Ah, but yours does. Did you ever live on Willoughby Avenue?"

"Yes…"

"And did you jump rope with that Irish girl, Mary Anne O'Shaughnessy?"

"Yes. Henry Katz?"

"Guilty!."

"I remember you," says Zenith. "You almost got hit by a cab, and If I recall correctly, you had an unfortunate bodily function accident as a result."

If a face could turn the color of the crimson Moroccan flag, mine is already there.

"Yes, that was sort of embarrassing," I say, looking for a way to disappear.

"We all had a laugh over that," she reminds me.

"Can we pretend that it didn't happen? I feel that it puts me at a competitive disadvantage."

"Sure," she giggles but apparently cannot. Becky shares in the frivolity. We are talking and laughing as my embarrassment slowly fades. Several of *Casablanca*'s patrons have finished dining and arrive at the hatcheck.

Becky waves me to the side, having received a coat check ticket from a large gentleman. My heart starts pounding violently as she hands him the very coat I took liberties with only moments before.

Becky helps the man on with his coat. I notice him patting the left pocket. The expression on his face changes from quite satisfied to bewilderment.

He re-pats that same pocket, then the right, and finally the inner one. The box he was sure was there, when he handed Becky the coat, no longer is.

"There is something missing from my pocket," he tells Becky, at first in a whisper. She returns a blank stare and raises her shoulders to show her ignorance of what might have transpired.

He repeats his claim, but this time far more forcefully. "Call the manager," he orders Becky.

Other patrons take notice and the area buzzes with excitement.

The distraught fellow moans about what appears to be the theft of the box he was convinced was in that side pocket before he sat down. This is a subtle hint that I should now be taking my leave.

I head for the door when I run into the *Maitre d'*, literally. It feels as though I just crashed into a wall. It was the suspicious Becky that summoned him. He is curious as to why I am in such a hurry to leave. I try slipping away, but a leg, comparable in size to a redwood log, trips me, sending me to the floor.

"Call the police," he shouts to Becky, who promptly complies.

I'm taken to a room and forced into a chair.

"Why da rush?" he asks in an accented voice. "Got a date?"

I guess I do now, I think, but not exactly the kind I had been expecting. The men in blue will be here momentarily.

Zenith Nadir is just plain bad luck, I think.

Chapter 31 • On the Road

"I don't like jail, they got the wrong kind of bars in there."

-Charles Bukowski

I'm in my cell, awaiting trial. Attempts by friends to raise money for bail have met with disappointment. There are worse places I could be, a synagogue or sitting next to an insurance salesman, come to mind.

Well, at least Edie and Sol are not here to learn of my misadventure. They're on the road heading for Florida to buy a place for retirement. She needs to get away from the New York winters, as her heart condition has worsened. I guess they'll find out about me eventually. Right now they're out of contact range, and even Sydney can't reach them. I guess that qualifies as a blessing—if anything can.

Last time we spoke they said they would be looking for a place in *alter cocker heaven*, AKA Fort Lauderdale. That should be great for Dad, who loves to play golf but never wants to spring for the bucks. This has gotten him into trouble with the private courses that discourage non-members from using their facilities. And dressing as he does, he doesn't quite fit in with the usual crowd, making him easy for security to spot.

He's not quite ready to retire; she is. And they want to see what they can look forward to in the next couple of years.

Images of Sol driving and Edie backseat driving come into my head. This, although a disturbing image, is not quite as bad as my fellow inmate about to relieve himself in our shared commode. I can just hear Edie telling Sol he's driving too slow, or coasting too much, while also reminding him how ugly his outfit is. Now I'm not sure whether I want to be there or here?

Only two weeks in this hellhole before my trial comes up. Gopher, the only lawyer I know, will be defending me. I expect to see him today so we can discuss the case. He's already warned me that my prospects are not looking good. Just the kind of encouragement you want to hear from your attorney.

I look around my cell, trying to avoid my temporary roommate who is struggling to release a stubborn turd while groaning in agony. What have I done to deserve this, I think, and then, oh, yeah—I remember.

There are no clocks within view, and we are required to surrender any jewelry before we are introduced to our new habitat. So I have no idea what time it is. Normally my stomach reminds me of approaching meal-times, but for some unexplainable reason, I'm not receiving those signals.

Just when things can't get much sicker, a guy dressed in kitchen garb arrives with two trays. I can hardly wait to see my sumptuous offering. I grab one tray, and Rufus—I think that's his name—goes for the other one. I uncover the tray to have a look and a whiff. "Want to exchange trays?" I ask my cellmate, imagining that by sheer magic, his would be superior.

With a grunt he hands his over, he too hoping in vain that he will be happier with the switch. This might have been possible if we had been served different elements of slop.

"What, no aperitif?" I ask, which is met by a blank stare.

Hours go by, and still no sign of Robert S. Broke, Esq. My choice for representation was either the Public Defender or Gopher Broke. Against my better judgment, I went with the latter. What the hell? How much worse can things really get? I am about to find out as the lockup guy tells me I've got a visitor.

I'm led to a private conference room where Gopher is already seated. Not that I expect anything different, but a gob of potato salad hangs off his chin and is about to drop onto his clipboard. I'm sure it will find a home in the company of all the other food stains already present.

"Hank. Babe. How goes it?" calls my attorney.

"Look around this place. How do you think *goes it*?"

"Okay, okay. This is just temporary."

"Oh, glad to know I'll soon be moving from here to a real prison."

"You are so negative. Have some faith, Babe."

"We both know that having faith is one of the many virtues I don't possess. Have you looked at my case?"

"Uh, I'm studying it now," says Bob, as his eye follow his finger down the page. It occasionally catches one of those gobs, which he quickly transfers to his tongue. "Oops, I don't think this tuna is from today," he comments.

After dozens of 'hmms' and 'ahhs,' he stops reading and looks up at my face, as I await his opinion.

"Not looking that good, Hank. I think they kind of have you by the balls. The box that was missing from that guy's coat was clearly in your possession when you tried to exit the restaurant. Maybe, if you hadn't made that mad dash you wouldn't have been a suspect."

"Thanks, Bob, but isn't it a little late for a lecture?"

"Not lecturing, Hank. Just giving you the facts. Just the facts, ma'am," he says in a poor imitation of Joe Friday. "It looks like your best shot is to plead guilty and say you were too drunk to know what you were doing.

That also might explain the imitation Rolex they found in your sock. Again, if you had worn the watch and not had it in your sock, that too might have allayed suspicion."

"What does this suggest, sentence wise?" I ask.

"You're looking at one to two. More if you plead not guilty and the D.A. unloads on you."

"So you're telling me to enroll myself in a state institution, and you don't mean *SUNY*."

"That's about it, Babe."

"Any other bad news you can provide," I ask, hoping that he wouldn't.

"Oh, yeah. What a schmuck. I almost forgot to tell you about the phone call I got from your sister last night."

"Sydney? Why did she call?"

"To ask me to let you know that your folks were in an automobile accident on their way down to Florida."

"Are they all right?" I ask with a panicked look.

"All I know is that their car was hit by an eighteen-wheeler, and Sydney's taking a bus down to Baltimore to try and see them."

"When were you going to tell me about this?" I screamed.

"I told you I was schmuck. Look, I'm really sorry. But you'll be comforted to know that they have no idea you're in the hoosegow."

It's several days later. Bob is scheduled to meet with me to let me know about the trial date. I'm taken to that private room where he sits, this time sans food stalactites from his chin. He doesn't look happy.

"Hank. Sit down. Take a breath."

"What is it? Say it." I implore.

"Your folks didn't make it."

Chapter 32 • Happy, Happy Birthday, Baby

"The most important rule for getting a birthday tattoo: if you want to show it to people, put it someplace where you won't have to take off your pants."

-Unknown

The generous folks at Bayview Correctional Facility Administration provided the 1974 wall calendar. I've been crossing off each passing day, in Magic Marker (pencils and pens are not provided because of their potential lethality), counting down the days to my release. I can see by that calendar that April 1st is coming and I'm about to celebrate my twenty-fourth birthday. I am also blissfully aware that this will be the only birthday party thrown in my honor at this wonderful institution. 'Celebration' may be too strong a term for a bunch of pierced, scarred, tattooed criminals singing "Happy Birthday" around the commissary lunch table, over platefuls of meat substance of questionable quality. What, no cake?

And what did I do to deserve a home in these luxurious quarters? Lifted a few wallets, slid a few *Rolexes* off of some unsuspecting wrists, 'explored' some pockets in a coatroom? It was that last one that put me in the clink.

Hatcheck girls get so antsy when complete strangers appear in their protected domains. They even go so far as to call the police. And judges have almost no senses of humor. So here I am, serving twelve months for petty theft (the *Rolex* had been a fake). If it were so petty, why am I in jail for it? Make up your God-dammed mind!

Twenty-four is an important milestone, because it is exactly one point one decades since the day I became a man, according to the Jewish faith. Who says I can't do complex math?

To participate in that ritual, called the *Bar Mitzvah* (sounds like a dude ranch in Galilee), I had to memorize a bunch of meaningless *Talmudic* text, called the *Haftorah*. Meaningless to me, to others, what ever floats your Ark.

I remember, with a great lack of fondness, my learning this gibberish, a ritual for Jewish boys reaching the ripe old age of thirteen. The ceremony included pledging one's devotion to the *alleged Supreme Being*. At my ceremony, I was relieved to hear that I could recite the entire spiel in Hebrew.

Since I learned it entirely by rote, having little understanding of the words I uttered, this made it much easier for a budding young "doubter" to participate in the sham.

The only thing happy about that event was the associated ritual of accepting envelopes from the guests, known as *Bar Mitzvah Gelt,* AKA: cash.

Little did I know that at the end of the evening of the reception, my mother would collect these envelopes from me—for 'safekeeping,' so I was told? I don't know what became of the money, but shortly after that Saturday, a shiny new Pontiac wagon was parked in front of our house.

So, only another month, and I am out of this only slightly improved version of *Hotel-6*, and it can't be too soon. After all, I have a life to catch up on, though I haven't the vaguest notion what I will do after offering my good-byes to fellow jailbirds and to those dedicated men in gray.

Of all the institutions in which I've been confined (including much of my public school education), this has not been one of my favorites. Federal prisons are supposed to be classier and attract more upscale tenants. I'll remember that the next time I'm again tempted to break the law.

Right now, I am on my best behavior. Don't want to risk a change of heart by the prison authorities. So, no more atheistic ranting, no vocal commentary on cell cleanliness or food quality.

Fred Kowalski is one of the guards assigned to my cellblock. He is not the brightest candle in the *Menorah*. In fact, it is rumored that when he is handed his Coke bottle at lunch, a little note appears on the bottom that says, "open other end." He has the intellectual capacity of a rhesus monkey, without the social graces. He grunts as he walks by, after I offer a "good morning, Officer K."

Kowalski and most of the other men in grey are suspicious by nature, but recent events have made them even warier. The incident in the cafeteria just yesterday contributed to this distrust. The alliteratively named Jesus Hernandez (pronounced 'Hey Soos'), serving three-to-five for automobile theft, tripped a guard as he walked past Hernandez' table. The *screw* (as guards are affectionately labeled by the convict population, dating back to the nineteenth century), Roman Kerinofski, fell over onto a table where some rather burly inmates were enjoying a delightful breakfast repast, spilling porridge all over their newly laundered orange jumpsuits. They pounced on the poor schmuck, resulting in genuine mayhem in the commissary, not to mention a treasure trove of gooey breakfast product as high up as the ceiling. Kowalski showed up to the rescue, billy club ready for action.

Jesus claims that the tripping was accidental, and who can argue with Jesus?

"How was I to know that he was gonna walk right were my foot was? I'm not a fucken mind reader," spake Jesus.

I am careful not to become involved in this incident. Any participation in rebellious activity would be judged harshly enough by prison authorities to put my release in jeopardy. But three days of solitary are rendered unto Jesus. I wonder if he'll rise to the occasion?

How a frail Jew, surrounded by brawny racists, sociopaths and sexually repressed horny toads, survives prison life for almost a year is a miracle, if, indeed, I actually believe in them.

The reason is owed to a most unlikely friend I made when I first arrived. Hemmet Young was the toughest, meanest looking son-of-a-bitch I ever laid eyes on, built like a bunker, with a shiny bald head casting a blinding reflection. On his face, a sandpaper beard that could be used in the carpentry workshop to smooth 2x4s. The giant swastika, tattooed on his neck, is pretty hard to miss. Inmates stay clear of him when passing. Some Bayview residents provide him with certain luxuries in exchange for his protection.

Hemmet is serving twenty-to-twenty-five for attempted murder, a crime he denies having committed, and maintains was a frame-up. I suppose he is not the first convict to make that claim. His bare hands can easily be used as murder weapons, but for some reason, I believed him.

Young is actually looking to reform. He's tired of the prison scene, and wanted to learn something that would enable him to become a legitimate member of society after doing his time. The swastika would not endear him to many potential employers, and one of the first things I "suggest" to him after he announces his ambition to go straight, is to rid himself of that ugly brand.

We spent time in the prison library, where I introduced him to literature and helped him understand the writing. He is far more intelligent than his hoodlum-like exterior makes him appear, and he learns quickly. My limited experience as a teacher is now paying off in ways I couldn't have imagined prior to my incarceration.

So, while any new inmate with buttocks faces the danger of unpleasant encounters with a sexually deprived stallion, my relationship with Hemmet protects me from these common attacks. The scuttlebutt (no pun intended) is that I am Hemmet's newest squeeze, but for reasons of self-preservation, this is never discussed in his presence—and it is also untrue.

April 1st. How appropriate that I was born on April Fools Day. The bell sounds, and cell doors slide open as criminals with hearty appetites flock to the commissary.

I sit down at my usual table—one considered to be privileged. Hemmet Young holds court here, and those who want or need to be part of his cadre strive to qualify for a seat.

Hemmet pounds the table with his fist, as a judge would with his gavel. Plates and cups jump up in response. "Have your attention, PLEASE," speaks his mighty voice.

Two inmates are deep in conversation at the other end of our table. Hemmet's fists come down again, this time creating a deep indentation in the tabletop. At this juncture, every eye and ear is on Hemmet. He motions to another inmate, dressed in the garb of kitchen staff. The man is carrying a tray of cupcakes, and lumbers over nervously, being extra careful not to drop any. There are eleven of these baked goodies, one for each guest, and an extra one for me. Well, it is my birthday. The tops of these cupcake babies are too small to accommodate any celebratory birthday decoration, not that the facility offers any to its guests. But somebody has managed to locate a small candle, albeit a previously used one, its remaining length less than an inch, plunged into the cupcake top.

"Make a wish," Hemmet commands, which is echoed by a half-dozen others. Inmates from other tables stare curiously in our direction. After all, it isn't every day that a glorious gala is held at *BCF*.

With any luck, my wish, to be anywhere but here, will soon be granted. I don't convey that desire audibly, so I won't insult my host, who obviously pulled some strings to make this event happen.

With eyes partially closed I say, "I wish that each and every one of you will be released long before your term expires, and that you will be successful on the outside, and never be stuffed in this dungeon again."

I then attempt to blow out the single, mere shadow of a former candle, only to see it reignite after each huff and puff. Obviously, it's a trick candle that can never be extinguished.

"Okay, who's the fuck'n wise guy?" yells Hemmet, standing ominously. Titters, coming from some of my tablemates, are quickly quelled. "I asked for a real candle for my friend's birthday, and someone thinks this is a joke?"

The candle-fetcher does not seem happy. He sweats as though he is about to be given testicular surgery without the benefit of anesthesia. And from all indications, that might just happen.

"S..sorry, H..hem," says commissary guy, quite nervously. "I must have t..taken the wrong c..candle out the drawer."

He is mercifully saved from the loss of his manhood by the sudden appearance of guard Kowalski, upon hearing louder-than-the-usual frivolity coming from our direction.

"Any problems, here?" asks Kowalski, eyeing the shaking commissary guy, and the seething Hemmet.

"N..No p..problem h..here," commissary guy assures the guard.

He returns to the kitchen, grateful that his ability to breed is still intact.

Glad that's over, I think, again concerned with my release—now only days away.

The singing of *Happy Birthday* begins, with those reluctant to participate "encouraged" by Hemmet's icy stare.

A prison first may have been achieved, as singing in the cafeteria had been heretofore unknown. I gaze at this unlikely chorus, noting that at least half are missing front teeth; all are tattooed in some fashion, and most bear permanent scars of unpleasant encounters with other criminals or members of law-enforcement.

When the song ends, Hemmet reaches for something in his pocket. All wince, expecting the worst, but their anxieties are calmed when he produces a small box wrapped in gift paper.

"Open it," he says, or rather, commands.

I fidget with the package, nervously trying to tear it open, wondering how Hemmet has obtained raffia ribbon. I have no idea what to expect, imagining that it might even contain a small derringer. Instead, it's a gold chain affixed to a crucifix.

I summon all the acting skills within me to convince Hemmet that the gift is something I've craved for years, though it doesn't quite fit my religious philosophy. Applause follows the unwrapping, and I bow to the group and thank Hemmet for his generosity. The group sings a chorus of *He's a Jolly Good Felon.*

Final arrangements are made. My old chum, Marty, will be waiting at the gate to drive me away from this joint, hopefully never to return. On my way down, I say my good-byes to a few of my fellow inmates, at least the ones who treated me somewhat decently. Kowalski grunts me his best wishes.

Hemmet's cell is next, and I pause in front of it. He looks up from a book on embroidery and acknowledges me standing there. He drops the book, stands up and embraces me fully. A tear forms in my eye, as this is a very touching moment. His hug would crush the former me, before those prison workouts added some heft to my frail frame.

"You gonna visit me like you promised?" he asks.

"Wouldn't dream of not visiting you," I affirm.

His head butts mine in a gesture meant to be friendly, but which leaves a red welt on my forehead. I pretend it doesn't hurt.

I stand before a clerk who has me sign a bunch of papers acknowledging the receipt of my personal effects, which include about eight hundred in cash. I earned it by being one of the best license plate producers in the joint. It's good to know that I now have a marketable skill that will take me places on the outside.

Chapter 33 • Splish Splash

"The first mistake in public business is going into it."

-Benjamin Franklin

Never volunteer for anything, and never go into retail—two sensible warnings that are seldom heeded. But sometimes a distinct lack of choices pushes you in a direction you don't want to go.

I'm sitting on a dilapidated sofa in my one room flat when the phone rings. It's close to ten p.m., and I make it a policy not to answer calls so late in the evening. In a moment of semi-consciousness, induced by a toke or three, I pick up the phone, without saying 'hello' or 'who the fuck is this calling me practically at midnight?'

"Henry?" speaks an unrecognizable voice.

"Yes, this is Henry, who's this?"

"It's your Uncle Ernie."

"Who?"

"Your uncle Ernie, Ernie Solomon. You must remember?"

"Ernie, Ernie, let's see. No, sorry. Are you sure you have the right number?"

"If you are Henry Katz, formerly of Crown Heights, Brooklyn, son of Edie and Sol Katz, I've got the right number. I've already called six other Henry Katzes, and yours is the last one left in the phone book."

The temptation to slam down the phone is halted by this identifying reference. My memory clears to remind me that I am a former Crown Heights resident, concluding that this is a person I might actually know. Now I remember. My long lost rich uncle!

"Uncle Ernie; sure. How the hell are you?"

"I'm surviving, and you?" he replies. Judging from that wad of cash he bestowed upon our family some fourteen or so years ago, unless he suffers a fate similar to mine, I'm thinking he's doing more than just surviving.

"Can you talk?" he asks. "Or do you want me to call you back at a better time? You sound a little woozy."

"Yes, you did wake me from a deep sleep," I lied. "But I'm fine. What's going on?"

"I'm about to make you an offer you can't refuse," he says.

"Oh, try me."

"As you may know, my fortune improves when others' fail. A business has come into my possession that I have no desire to run, but it's in a wonderful location-location-location, and has a great chance of success, with the right person at the helm."

In my stupor I ask, "What kind of business?"

"It's a retail store on the Upper West Side."

"You want me to work in a retail store?" I ask, incredulously.

"Not work—manage!"

"Wait a second. You want me to manage a store? My only retail experience was selling electronics at *Looney Louie's*, although, I was their number one salesman."

"That's just the kind of person I'm looking for, someone who knows how to sell, but has no preconceived management notions. Judging from the number of closed stores I'm seeing lately, there doesn't seem to be much sound business judgment out there."

"Uncle Ernie, I don't know…"

"You don't have to answer now, but I want you to think about a salary of thirty k, a bonus based on profit and a chance to own it after you prove to me that I have not made a terrible mistake."

"Well, let me think about it. Can I call you tomorrow?"

"Of course, take your time, but I will need to know by Monday."

I squint at the calendar hanging on the wall, and see that I have three days in which to make up my mind.

"I'd like to see the store before going any further."

"Sure thing," he says, and provides me with the address, which sounds vaguely familiar, along with his phone number for the call back. I jot them down without looking at the sheet of paper.

I awaken early the next morning and ponder the possibilities. I assume that the conversation with my uncle actually happened, and I hadn't just dreamt it.

Let's see. My Uncle Ernie, an attorney who specializes in business fore-closures, has obtained a property that went into default. I hadn't seen Ernie since my *Bar Mitzvah*, where I recall he handed me quite a sizeable sum, which my mother quickly grabbed for 'safekeeping.' Like the other funds collected that day, I never saw a penny of it, but Edie constantly mentioned it whenever she discussed her only rich relative.

Why he thought of me when this "opportunity" came along, I'll never know, but he must have remembered my stellar performance in the read-ing of the *Haftorah* or deduced from the demise of *Looney Louie's* that I might be looking for work. I don't know how he even knew that I had been employed there.

The address is a long walk from my dingy little abode, but I can use the exercise, and certainly can't afford a cab. I think about getting a decent apartment with the money that I could be making if I take Ernie up on his offer.

I arrive on the block where the store is located. It finally hits me that Er-nie's store is the former *Looney Louie's*. "That's why this address sounds so familiar," I say to myself.

Business in this neighborhood appears to be flourishing. There are plen-ty of *Upper Westsiders* out and about—lots of baby carriages, and taxis discharging passengers who head into local stores.

The building has a **STORE CLOSED** sign hanging on the boarded up window.

Painful memories are summoned upon seeing the former electronics store. Looney Louie (not his actual name) got in trouble with the law for using bait and switch advertising practices. He was also convicted for buying stolen property and reselling it at insane prices. He never had any of the merchandise he advertised on the radio. His slogan, "Go nuts at Looney Louie's, because his prices already are," was repeated multiple times daily on almost every radio station in New York.

Simon Mizrahi, AKA Looney Louie, knew every trick in the book, and turned hustling into an art form. He would have been comfortable at a rug bazaar in his parents' homeland in the heart of Aleppo, Syria. He would always quote triple the price the merchandise was actually worth, with the full expectation that the customer would counter his offer for only double what he actually expected to get for it. He appeared to be insulted when the customer tried to bargain, and Simon was a master at guilt tripping.

"It's alright," he'd tell the bargainer, "My baby doesn't really need to eat this week."

Mizrahi hired me after he fired practically his entire staff for stealing a good chunk of his inventory. They didn't believe that robbery committed against a thief was immoral. And if you take the coolie wages he paid them into consideration, their assessment of him was not far off.

This was not my first employment choice, but after my little stint at the correctional institution, recruiters were not exactly knocking down my door.

I'm having second thoughts about working here again, although it would not be for Mizrahi. He's currently enjoying a semi-private room at a correctional facility, serving a fifteen-year sentence.

I'm about to turn around and head home when I look up to see Uncle Ernie smiling from ear-to-ear. "Henry," he calls out to me. "What do you think?"

"Sorry, Unk," I say. "I have no desire to go into the electronics business again."

"Not electronics, but a bed and bath store. We could be the next *Bed Bath and Beyond*, without the Beyond."

"A bath shop?" I ask incredulously. "What do I know about shower curtains?

"Have no fear. My wife, Julie, was a buyer at *Gimbels* and knows everything about bath products. She really misses her life there, and might get some vicarious pleasure by helping you along. Besides, according to your mother, you spend a good deal of time in the bathroom, so you must be an expert."

I don't quite understand how my onanistic ritual could lend itself to bathroom merchandise expertise. Still, the idea is intriguing.

My question now is how does a former history teacher, who has served time in a County facility, use that experience to manage a toilet seat business? It isn't as if I have no retailing background. Besides Looney Louie's, I did work in an appetizing store as a kid. There was also the pharmacy.

The schoolyard gig didn't quite work out, resulting from the failure of my perfume procurement technique. The manager had a problem with some of his merchandise finding its way into my socks. Picky-picky.

"Do you have a name for this enterprise?" I ask.

"I'll leave that up to you," he says.

The idea of running a bath store begins to grow on me. And having executive control—wow! Even better than ordering Teddy Finkle around during our rocket-building days.

We arrange to have dinner at his house where I can meet his wife, Julie. I will be meeting her for the first time. Ernie's first wife, who had accompanied him to my Bar Mitzvah, has since passed away.

The evening goes well. Ernie has conveniently forgotten to mention my prison record, and Julie and I get along just fine, she having no preconceived notions about me. Julie has a wealth of knowledge about merchandising in general, and the products our store will soon be selling, in particular. Being confined to a wheelchair, resulting from an accident on a *Gimbel's* escalator, will make it difficult for her to appear at the store very often, but she will help with the design and educate me on product.

"How does the *Splish Splash Shop* sound?" I ask Ernie and Julie.

"Well your father used to tell you that you were all wet, so it sort of fits," says Ernie, who apparently was more privy to our family conversations than I was aware of.

After a month and a half of construction, our merchandise begins to pour in. We have created a shower curtain department larger than any in town. I call it the *Great Wall*, only sorry that we are not carrying china in our store.

Our towel department sparkles with the latest colors from *Fieldcrest Mills*. We have a selection of toilet seats that even *Macy's* would envy. They are made in an array of materials: solid oak, hard and soft plastic, laminated wood and even faux-fur. I order a sign saying, "We Stand Behind Our Toilet Seats, So You Can Stand in Front of Them." Julie is not in favor of this sign, commenting, "We would never have done that at *Gimbels*."

Today I'm interviewing sales and stock people, and will try to choose a qualified assistant manager from the candidates. I have an opening target date of September 5th, giving me about ten days to staff the store and train the employees.

In walks a young Asian girl, about four-foot ten, wearing a tight little skirt. She has a smile that can render a hypnotic spell. I try not to let this obvious temptation cloud my thinking. Mai Ling Wu tells me she's from Hong Kong, in a thick yet charming accent. She attends college in the evenings, and can work a full-time schedule during the day. She is also available on weekends, which is a requirement for the job. I'm definitely seeing her as a candidate for the assistant manager position. I will have to interview a whole lot of other people before I can come to a decision.

The next person sent by the employment agency is a tall, stocky man of about thirty with thick, curly hair. Ashour Haqq approaches me with his hand outstretched. He smiles revealing several gold teeth. He speaks with a faint Arabic accent, and seems quite enthusiastic. He has worked for a retailer that sold similar products.

"And why did you leave your former employer," I ask.

"*Jewish lightning*," he replies.

"Excuse me?"

"*Jewish lightning*," he repeats, smiling. "I don't mean to sound prejudiced. If fact, I am married to a Jewish woman. It is a term to define a fire that begins under mysterious circumstances, particularly when the business is losing money."

"Ah," I reply, now aware that the meaning of that phrase was not what I originally thought.

It's the end of the second day of interviews. We now have a staff ready to train, three full-timers and five part-timers—in a mix of races and genders.

I have read my *Instant Manager* thoroughly, picking up tips on managing people effectively. I learned what wasn't obvious to Looney Louie: compliment publicly, chastise privately. Find something good to say about an employee, and say it. From a variety of sales training manuals I get: teach them to look the customer in the eye, and smile like you are their best friend; don't tell customers that every product in the store is terrific. Criticize an item to establish your credibility. Selling is psychology. "Visualize how your guests will feel when they enter your bathroom, and your shower curtain enthralls them."

The big day arrives. I have cleaned up my act, and no longer wake up in the woozy state to which I was accustomed. This new apartment is quite an improvement over the standing-room-only place I just vacated. Ernie insisted that I move as soon as possible after I described my slum to him in detail. A nice cash advance enabled a noticeable wardrobe improvement as well. And the icing on he cake, the apartment is only three blocks from the store.

I arrive before eight a.m., to two *Grand Opening* signs that are emblazoned on the store's windows. I'm expecting my staff to arrive by nine, providing us with an opportunity for a one-hour dry run.

While waiting for the staff, I perform the usual management duties: worry, check the a/c, ensure that all displays are lit, worry, load the cash register, worry, verify that our credit card machine works flawlessly. Did I mention worry? I can take the time remaining until store opening to twiddle my thumbs. I'm far too nervous to read the newspaper I brought with me, so twiddling it will be.

It's now nine twenty-five. Not one employee has arrived—so much for a lengthy dry run. I begin to perspire profusely. What if nobody shows up?

What if customers show up and the staff doesn't? Or visa versa? Which would be worse?

Finally my team starts filtering in, beginning with Mai Ling, then Lamont, our *Supply Associate* (the dignified title I created for 'stock clerk'). Monty sports an Afro—tall enough to house a colony of bees. Finally Tamisha enters, begging forgiveness for her late arrival. She and Mai Ling will begin as sales associates and we'll see where it goes from there. They wear competing mini-skirts, with legs to match. This completes our opening staff, much to my relief.

I make a mental note to remind these people that I hold their start times sacred. Lateness will not be tolerated. I don't want to get off on a bad footing, so I'll save that reprimand for a later time.

It's now ten minutes of ten. Crowds are beginning to form outside the door, some of them carrying our flyer in their hot little hands.

Rrrrrrrrring!

Our opening bell goes off just in case any of our people are asleep. We take our positions in the store, ready as we'll ever be, to interact with our customers. I stand behind the register, faking a smile as they enter. Lamont stands ready to fetch heavy items such as a hamper or doctor's scale from the basement when that need arises.

"Welcome to *Splish Splash*," I shout each time another customer crosses the threshold.

Chapter 34 • Joys of a Shopkeeper

"The key to being a good manager is keeping the people who hate me away from those who are still undecided."

-Casey Stengel

Neil Something is a frequent customer. He stands at about 5 foot 11, bad rug, New York accent—probably the Bronx, Jewish mannerisms, but Italian last name. He's got absolutely no taste. Neil requires a minimum of three people to agree on which shower rings to buy. He will ask everyone in the general area around the counter if they approve of his choice, including the homeless man that comes in to collect empty soda bottles.

He constantly mentions the girl that is coming to live with him, who remains nameless. Do we think she'll like the shower curtain he is considering buying? It's kind of sexy, right? Or is it too sexy! Will it go with the nude drawings he is purchasing (or contemplating purchasing)? These are small pictures—about 5x7 inches. He is not sure whether to buy them because he doesn't have anyone to put them up for him. Banging in a picture hook is considerably beyond his carpentry skills.

His girlfriend, he again reminds us, is coming to live with him. He has been telling us for months, about this girl from New Jersey, who is coming to live with him. She must be coming by way of Kalamazoo, and limping.

We would all love to meet this woman.

The shower curtain being considered has been in the clearance section for the past eight months and has been marked down at least six times. Two charities turned it down.

Neil, worrying about his girlfriend's sensibilities—and concerned that he will have difficulty in taking the old curtain down—ponders the decision.

A well-dressed, very attractive woman, merchandise in hand, moves to the register to complete her purchase. Neil shows the woman every item in the store he has bought from us, or is thinking about buying.

He tells her everything that is currently in his bathroom, including its plumbing problems. Neil probably should have avoided the part about the toilet backup after his morning's first bowel movement. He seeks the benefit of her wisdom before making these next few choices.

I watch from the distance, pretending to be talking on the phone, so I can avoid dealing directly with him. I cringe, gripping my hands into as much of a prayer pose as a secularist can muster, as Neil pops the question to the female shopper.

"Pleeese don't blow it," I beg to myself. The shopper notices me cringing, and somehow senses my need.

"No, I don't think that it's too wild," she assures him as she studies the design—female California raisins, dancing on a stage. They are attired in very low cut dresses.

"But my girlfriend from New Jersey is coming to live with me. Do you think she'll find it too provocative?" Neil inquires.

"Neil," I yell from the behind the telephone, "If she's from New Jersey, she'll love it," sparing the on-the-spot customer from having to answer.

"That happens to be the best-selling shower curtain in New Jersey," I continue, obviously very anxious to make this sale. "Besides, who's King in your castle?"

This reasoning seems to do the trick, as Neil fumbles for his wallet. Getting orange, green and shocking pink towels to match this shower curtain will be a problem to attack at a later date.

It's five past ten on a Saturday morning, busiest day of the week. Here's a chance to make up for some of the clinkers we've had early in the week.

None of the staff has arrived. We cannot open the store without at least one other staff member.

The gate remains down as potential patrons wait outside, nervously looking at their watches. One couple gives up and walks away. I motion to the remaining shoppers, putting up a "two minutes" sign with the fore and middle fingers. They acknowledge with a "one"—and guess which finger? Finally, they leave, perhaps preferring to shop in a store that is actually open.

Just then the staff begins to arrive. "Sorry," says Mai Ling, who travels in on the Flushing line.

Lena arrives two minutes later. She was hired soon after we had to let Tamisha go.

Lena's commute consists of a walk from two doors down the street. "Miss the ten o'clock elevator?" I hiss.

"Very funny, I'm three minutes late. What's the big deal?"

"We go by our clock", argues the boss, "which makes you eight minutes late."

She doesn't hear me, because she has already exited the store to get a container of coffee. I have the feeling that I don't have complete control.

Now that the staff is finally all here, the customers are not. I wait fifty-five minutes for the first one to walk in.

She carries a bag with the store's markings, which means that our first transaction will undoubtedly be a return.

"Good morning," I say—gritting my teeth. "How can we help you this morning?"

"I'd like to return this toilet seat," she whines. "My husband hates it!"

I wonder what kind of husband would hate a pink toilet seat with orange butterflies painted on it that I thought I was finally rid of.

This seat was sold to us by a vendor who charmed me into buying it, against my better judgment. Who says wise decision making trumps a mini-skirt and low-cut top? But the saleswoman was exotic and used provable sales techniques. Those suggestive lips and eyes did the rest.

But, I digress. A while back, this design was part of the *Mariposa* collection, a successful group of items by a now defunct manufacturer.

The company advertised it with such catchy phrases as "Turn your bathroom into a spring garden…" This was during a time when you could not have enough butterflies. It had matching towels, rugs, shower curtains, bathroom scales, porcelain bath accessories, and of course, this toilet seat. All the other pieces eventually sold at the 'right' price, but the seat was a little more stubborn.

"Ma'am, didn't the salesperson explain to you that this would be a final sale?" I query. "After all it was marked down from forty dollars to a dollar ninety-nine."

"Definitely not!" was the indignant reply. "I asked the salesgirl if I could take it home and try it, and she said 'sure.'"

"Is that salesperson here right now?" I ask, attempting to smile my way through this painful inquiry.

"Yes," she says, "Its the one over there drinking coffee," pointing to Lena.

"Does your husband realize that this is a collector's item that could be worth a lot of money, someday?" I ask while trying to keep a straight face.

"Could I just have a refund, please," asserts the woman. "I'm a very good customer in this store."

"Do you have a receipt, and the original box," I ask—knowing full well that she has neither.

"Who saves those?" is the reply.

"How you can pass up this item, which obviously should have been marked ten times higher, is beyond me. Well I'm glad to get it back. Mai Ling, mark this seat eighty dollars and put it back in stock." I say, refunding the dollar ninety-nine plus tax.

The satisfied customer walks out, as I yank at a few follicles on my head, the hairline of which is already beginning to recede. I pick up the seat, and smash it to the floor, tossing the remains into the trash pit.

"There. That's a sure-fire way to get rid of a collector's item," I exclaim, not all that quietly.

Chapter 35 • Have a Ball

"Sometimes it's not how good you are, but how bad you want it"

-Unkonwn

It's *Splish Splash*'s first anniversary. We've actually survived in the retail business for one whole year, calling for a celebration. I have arranged for a party to be held at a billiard hall, not far from here. I was able to rent the entire place for the evening, with Ernie's blessing—and he volunteered to pay the tab.

The store will be closing in just a few minutes and we will head over to *It's Your Cue* for our party. Our entire staff is invited along with their better (or worse) halves. Ernie and wife will be present, but I'm not expecting any professional level eight ball from Julie, as her wheelchair could be an inhibiting factor. Several of our favorite vendors were extended invitations, which most have accepted. I also invited Marty and Gopher, and appealed to them not to be more of an embarrassment to me than they absolutely have to.

I asked Gretta, the woman I met recently as the result of a Personals ad in *New York Magazine*. She told me she hopes to be here, but business priorities could prevent her appearance. I'm really hoping she'll make it. She's quite a knockout, and I'd sure love to show her off.

Mai Ling asked her boyfriend to join us, and the two make a cute little couple (neither is over five feet tall). She was promoted to assistant manager about a month after the store opened. Unfortunately, her rival for the position, Tamisha Rogers, was fired for stealing, a week into her service. I was sorry to see those legs go, but even sorrier to see our best-selling items go without benefit of a cash register ring.

I'm happy to once again get my hands on a cue stick. It's time to concentrate on the game, and let worrying about the store rest for the night.

I challenge my uncle to a game of nine-ball. He swears he hasn't played in years, and then asks if I want to make it interesting. I'm suspicious, having been hustled once or twice before.

"Okay, what stakes," I ask.

"Tell you what," he says. "Beat me two out of three and *Splish Splash* is all yours."

"Uncle Ernie. Am I hearing you correctly?"

"You heard right. Win two nine-ball games from me, and I will give you the store."

I was already aware of my uncle's generosity, but I'm flabbergasted by his willingness turn the whole caboodle over to me after only a year of operation.

"But Hank, you do have to win two out of three," he reminds me.

"And if I lose?"

"You pay the check for tonight's party," he says.

So I have an opportunity to own my own business, one that I've taken a shine to. All I have to do is win two games in the only sport I'm actually good at. And if I lose, it costs me a grand or so.

"You're on, Unk."

My hand is shaking—not the best condition for winning a game of pool, and changing my life….

Ernie wins the lag for break, and breaks open the pack with a powerful shot that can be heard throughout the establishment. Three balls go down—an impressive start. He makes the first ball and misses the next one.

My turn. I can't seem to stop that nervous hand.

"Relax," he says. "This is only for the store."

"Yeah, thanks, Unk. That settles me down."

My shiny new cue quakes in my hand. "Steady…" I tell myself. "Breathe, deep breaths," I say, and finally calm down sufficiently to have enough confidence for my first shot. "*WPA* rules?"

"Yep," he confirms. "We play by *World Pool Association* rules applied to scratches and penalties."

Uncle Ernie left me a mess. I survey the table for an odd chance that I have a shot at striking the number two ball. My first shot is going to have to be a jumper, if I am to avoid a scratch. The blue ball is almost at the end of the table from where I must shoot. I don't have to make the two, only touch it to avoid the penalty, otherwise giving a ball-in-hand advantage to my uncle. I line up the shot, and after several feints and withdrawals, I'm ready to shoot. I close my eyes and boom—thar she blows. I don't open them until I hear the welcoming sound of a click at the other end. Not only have I hit the two ball, but it has also knocked in two others.

Cheers break out from spectators I hadn't realized were even watching. Unbeknownst to me, Ernie passed the word on what the stakes of the game were, thus drawing much more than the usual crowd.

I keep possession of the cue until just two numbered balls remain on the table. In nine-ball, one can almost run the table and still be defeated, missing the remaining ball. I am now facing increasing odds against seeing the six, partially obscured by the eight. As I anticipated, the blockage prevents me from scoring, giving Uncle Ernie an easy victory for game number one.

"I guess you don't want the store," he says with a grin from ear to ear. "Now, all you have to do is win the next two. That shouldn't be a problem for Hank the hustler."

Now I wonder who is being hustled. Did he just set me up for a major disappointment, not to mention the bill at the end of the night?

Somehow, I'm able to win game number two, despite trailing the way he did in the first game.

Now it's the money game. There is enough moisture in my armpits to start my own reservoir. By now, all the other tables in the joint are abandoned as twenty or so guests surround ours.

Ernie breaks the pack with a crashing shot that sends the one, three and eight into corner pockets. He continues shooting with precision until only five feet of space separates the cue ball from the nine. Only a palsied hand could mess up his chance to sink it; ending the game and my hopes.

"Nine in the side," he calls, as dictated by the rules. He confidently shoots and somehow misses, putting me back into the game. I'm suspicious. He really wants me to have the store, I think. "Who am I to disappoint," I say loud enough for all to hear. I easily down the nine after calling the shot. It's Your Cue comes alive with screaming cheers.

The next thing I know is that I'm sitting at a table with the smiling former owner of *Splish Splash* and Julie, his lovely wife. A bottle of champagne is brought to the table along with three glasses. Other glasses are filled for the various employees and other invitees.

Uncle Ernie stands to salute the new owner of *Splish Splash*, and delivers a warm good luck speech for the entire crowd to hear. Cheers are heard all around as bottles of champagne are quickly downed.

"We looked at your numbers, Julie and I, "says Ernie. "We agreed that you have done a fine job with *Splish* and are worthy of ownership. That may have accounted for my amateurish play at then end of game three."

"May have accounted?" I volunteered.

Suddenly a hush comes over the entire billiard hall. Julie has slumped over in her seat, dropping her champagne glass onto the carpet. Ernie rushes over to tend to his wife. He calls her name several times without response. He grabs her wrist to feel for a pulse—finding none. "Is there a doctor in this place?" he shouts to no avail.

Finally someone calls 9-1-1. We wait for the arrival of the emergency medical response team, but it is obvious that it is a hearse—not an ambulance, that is required.

Chapter 36 • Taxman

"Death, taxes and childbirth! There's never any convenient time for any of them."

-Margaret Mitchell, Gone with the Wind

It seems like only yesterday that I computed my federal income tax for the year my favorite group recorded *Revolver*. And here I am, sitting in the outer sanctum of the Manhattan office of the *Department of Internal Revenue*.

I look around and observe the five others also waiting to be called in for what is euphemistically referred to as an interview. Most are quiet, fearful and nervous. A man sitting opposite me is dressed in ultra-orthodox garb; a long winter coat (it is July), and a fur-trimmed *huckel* (hat) embellishes his heavily bearded face, with curly *payos* hanging from it. A pair of canvas shoes completes the look (leather is forbidden in orthodox dress). He rocks back and forth, as muffled Hebrew words pour from his mouth. He is doubtlessly praying that his return will not be examined too closely when his time arrives. Though he is a man of God, it appears that he may have lost confidence that Yahweh has granted full approval of his tax computation methodology.

Only the guy sitting to my right is feeling talkative. He introduces himself, despite my head being buried in a book, and not appearing to be in need of company.

"So, they got you, too, eh?" he asks.

I pretend that I'm hearing impaired and ignore him, hoping he will die, or at least shut up and leave me alone.

He extends a hand as if to shake, but then turns over his calling card, indicating that he is in the insurance business. "Name's Hochstein," he says, a smile beaming across his face.

I'm thinking this is an odd place to be hawking insurance. I turn away as he continues talking. I pray, as much as my religious proclivities will permit, that he will get the hint. His breath resembles the stench of a decomposing corpse, a further reason to face in another direction. I am imagining Hochstein being greeted by the *IRS* agent, and immediately pitching a whole-life policy.

A door marked "Chambers" opens and a curly-haired man with a polka-dot bow tie and thick horn-rimmed glasses calls, "Bronstein? Myron Bronstein."

The rocking motion ceases and the very tall orthodox man pulls himself up and approaches the door. He's at least three heads taller than Mr. Curly Head. Neither man is smiling.

I watch as the *Hassid* leaves the room, thinking that I am probably next. Mr. Hochstein, or me, I hope. I begin to imagine what might be behind that door. A picture of an *Inquisitor* comes into my mind, wearing fifteenth century religious garb with huge cross embroidered across his chest. Torches flicker on walls, next to men hanging upside down. The screams of rack-stretched sinners fill the room. I'm thinking, "what would they do to you if you took two extra deductions?"

Hochstein has not given up. "You still haven't told me why you're here," demands the insurance guy. "You can trust me. All my clients do, and it has served them well."

Just when I am about to tell Hochstein to have sex with himself, but not in a fun way, the door opens again, and a *cafe au lait*-complected woman calls my name. I never dreamed being beckoned by the *IRS* could be a welcome occurrence.

"Please come in, Mr. Katz," she says, motioning me in with her clipboard.

"I'm Agent Miriam Klenda-Jones. I see that you are not represented by an accountant or an attorney."

This is not a greeting I'm particularly happy to hear. I am ushered to a chair, and she takes her seat behind the desk.

She shuffles a bunch of official-looking papers, and stares up at me periodically—uttering "hmm" every couple of seconds. All I can do as she goes through my file is to look around the room, noticing its sparse decor. A photo of herself and three handsome young children sits in a frame on her desk. No man is present in this family picture. Her current Afro is decidedly fuller than the one she sports in the photo.

"Nice looking family," I say.

"Uh huh," she replies, which, translated, means, "I ain't buying."

After several quite uncomfortable minutes pass, she puts down the file and stares into my face with eyes that could do the work of Bunsen burners. I fidget, waiting for her to let loose. After all, I do know why I'm here.

"Mr. Katz…"

"Please, call me Hank," I interrupt.

"Mr. Katz," she continues, ignoring my sincere gesture of friendliness. "I've been assigned your case file—after some, er, irregularities were flagged."

"Irregularities?"

"Uh, let's just call them that."

I have, in this file, your Federal Returns for the years 1976 and 77."

She slides both returns toward me and asks, "Is that your signature on these documents?"

I study the signatures with great scrutiny, as if there is some question as to whether I signed them. After three minutes of finger tapping, the impatient Agent Klenda-Jones pulls them from my hands, looking not particularly happy.

"It was a simple question, Mr. Katz. Did you, or did you not, sign these returns?"

"Well, they do look like my signature," I reluctantly affirm.

"According to these returns, *Splish Splash Emporium* had expenses that well exceeded revenues, let alone profit."

"That enterprise, unfortunately, has not been as successful as I had first predicted. Also, the expenses associated with the business were much greater than I originally anticipated."

"Yes, we noticed that as well. We also noticed that you show an entry for a fire inspector bribe to the tune of twenty thousand."

"Agent Klenda-Jones," I say. "I may not be a lawyer, but I do know that the bribery of a city official is not a federal offense, and is a basic part of doing business in New York."

The agent's cold stare accompanies the statement, "You also made a deduction for restaurant supplies and equipment totaling over ninety thousand dollars. When we visited your premises we could find no restaurant or coffee bar within your store."

"Yes, I thought that was kind of a weird expense when I signed that check, but when you're busy-busy-busy, you don't have a lot of time for details. I pointed our accountant toward the door, after that one."

You see, the problem about trying to sidestep *IRS* simple rules and regulations is that they don't take kindly to them. Even a relatively minor infraction can create enough suspicion to engender a full investigation of all of your previously submitted returns. And when they don't find one for several reporting years, it piques their interest even further.

When agent Klenda-Jones first slid those returns toward me, I was relieved that 1975 did not come up in conversation. That relief did not have longevity, not because the returns were full of errors, but that they didn't exist.

Who knew that you're supposed to submit these every single year?

The short of it is that I am guilty of income tax evasion. I'm in violation of Federal Statute 7201, under Title 26, whatever that means. This rule states that violators are subject to imprisonment, fines, or both.

So, I'm here in this courtroom, watching snowflakes the size of baseballs pelting the windows, while I sit and wait for the arrival of Judge Francis Lincoln to take his place on what is called "the Bench." You'd think that a judge should at least be provided with something more comfortable upon which to plop his derriere, but no. This could explain the mood most judges seem to share when it is time to decide on the fate of the accused.

I'm cognizant of the fact that my lifelong friend and attorney, Robert S. Broke, Esq., has not yet arrived. I'm hoping he makes his appearance before His Honor does, because Judge Lincoln is known to become upset when a defendant's attorney is not present for the reading of the charges. I look around hoping to spot him, but instead make eye contact with Agent Klenda-Jones. I shoot her a weak smile, which is returned by a look of abject disgust.

Perhaps my decision-making was impaired when I elected to name Gopher to defend me, instead of some court-appointed schmuck. At least this was a schmuck I knew.

I'm relieved to see Gopher bursting through the double doors, panting.

"Sorry," he calls out, alerting the entire courtroom to his grand entrance. He approaches the accused's table with a ratty old briefcase in one hand, and a greasy, brown paper bag in the other. Directly behind him is the bailiff, shouting words like, "Sir, you may not bring food into the courtroom."

Gopher takes a massive bite out of what remains of his sandwich, a practically impossible to believe quantity of food shoved almost directly down his throat. "Sorry," he tells the bailiff, showering him with particles of chicken salad and a spray of mayonnaise.

The bailiff tears the soggy bag from Gopher's hand, and dumps it into the trash basket next to our table, brushing the detritus off of his uniform blouse while trying to keep his dignity intact.

"Where the hell have you been?" I ask Gopher. "Chasing more ambulances?"

"Sorry," he utters for what is now the third time, and the only word out of his mouth since his arrival.

I'm hoping that he won't be using that as part of our defense. "Have you reviewed the case?" I ask, confident that the answer would be "no."

"Not as yet," he replies. "But trust me. I know how to handle these judges."

"Trust you? Not as yet? When would you say would have been the appropriate time?"

My question must have been heard by most of the courtroom, as a multitude of stares focus in our direction.

"Hear Ye, Hear Ye," cries the bailiff. "Federal Court, District 19 is now in session, the Honorable Francis Lincoln presiding. All stand."

Judge Lincoln waves us all to take our seats. He is a distinguished looking man of color, resplendent in his black robe and very expensive silk tie. I assume he does not shop at *Kleins on the Square*.

"The defendant, Henry A. Katz, residing at 142 1/2 West 74th Street, Manhattan, is accused of violating Section Blah blah, Title blah blah, of the Federal Income Tax Code," comes the baritone voice of His Honor. "Is counsel present?"

"Yes, your honor," my attorney shouts as a torrent of bread crumbs cascades down from his trousers as he stands up. "Robert S. Broke, Esq., counsel for the defense."

"How do you wish to plead?"

"Guilty with an explanation, your honor."

I'm thinking, is it too late to get that public defender?

"Please proceed."

The ball is now in our court, and I can only hope that we do a lot better than our performance in our last judicial doubles match.

Chapter 37 • Desperate Measures

"Creditors have better memories than debtors."

-Ben Franklin

Things have not gone so well since "winning" the store from Uncle Ernie. It's almost as if Devine Providence waited until he signed ownership over to me before striking. Even though I don't believe in that hogwash, every once in a while, and with encouragement from that pain-in-the-ass voice, I think it would be a good idea to stop cursing the alleged Supreme Being—or that He is even alleged.

When Ernie still controlled the purse strings, he would supplement our bank account when we closely missed our figures. We usually made it up in the succeeding months.

Now it seems that our sales figures are falling every day. The phone is ringing off the hook with vendors looking to get paid for past due invoices. When I answer those calls, I pretend I'm the stock boy—not that much of a stretch since I was forced to let Lamont go.

A visit from our commercial trash collector's goon squad hasn't helped. They showed up demanding a huge increase in collection fees. When informed that I was not in a position to pay their new rates, they shot me a look that was meant to strike terror.

"I would figure out a way to come up with the money, Mr. Katz," said the tallest and meanest of the three. "Otherwise, things of an unpleasant nature might begin to happen." His two companions nod in agreement.

Might begin to happen? I thought. I bear the look of a condemned man facing a firing squad. "I'll see what I can do," I lie, knowing that under present conditions I can barely cover my payroll. The only thing in my favor is that Uncle Ernie is offering me a ridiculously low monthly rent. If market rates applied, I would have gladly lost that nine-ball game.

Not able to offer any raises to my employees result in two of the best ones leaving, and others either liberating the cash register when no one was watching, or pilfering goods from the shop. This is obviously payback for my drugstore days.

It's a weekday morning and I'm in my office working with my accountant, Lou. Prompted by the latest employee thievery, my friend Billy mounted for me, only two nights before, a hidden camera to monitor what goes on near the register. I do not like what I'm seeing. My little China doll assistant manager is removing cash from the drawer. There are no customers, so the cash is not to make change. I brusquely excuse myself to Lou and practically fly out my office door.

Mai Ling is bending over to fill a towel shelf from an open drawer and senses me leaning over her.

"Mai Ling, please come with me."

She stands up startled. Her normally beautiful complexion begins glowing red. I call one of the other employees over to watch the front of the store, and hasten Mai Ling toward the office.

"What is problem?" she asks.

"I'll show you," I say, in a not very pleasant voice.

Lou knows what's coming and steps out of the small office to make room. She is shocked to see the monitor on the wall of my office. I re-run the tape to display her criminal act. She's given a choice of returning the cash she just took, or facing arrest. She chooses the former, hastily making for the door without a goodbye to fellow employees, including her best friend, Mei Ying, who had been hired on Mai Ling's recommendation.

I am devastated. I thought the world of Mai Ling, never suspecting that she would steal from me. "If I can't trust her, who can I?" I wonder. A mental note is made to keep my eye on Mei Ying, wondering if she will continue in her friend's footsteps.

In the absence of help to perform menial tasks I've added to my own chore list, sweeping the sidewalk outside the storefront twice daily. This is legal requirement for all merchants in the city. It's usually a lesson in futility because this is such a busy street, inhabited and invaded by litterbugs. I finish the task, ensuring that the curb is swept in compliance with the code.

I'm back behind the register. My keen eyes sweep the store for criminal activity, now suspicious of everyone.

Mei Ying approaches and asks me, "Did Mai Ling leave store because she sick?"

"Better ask her yourself, Mei Ying, but I'm not at liberty to discuss it." She looks at me quizzically, half understanding what I just said.

The copper bell at the front door indicates someone just entering. "Oh, good," I say to no one but me, "must be a customer returning something."

But to my chagrin, it is a uniformed sanitation officer, with a clipboard. "Are you da managuh?" he asks in a crisp *Bronxonian* accent.

After I reply in the affirmative he hands me a summons from the clipboard, telling me I'm in violation of NYC Administrative Code. Also now in my hand is a brochure describing all of the provisions of the code.

"I'm familiar with the code, and not less than ten minutes ago, I was out there with a broom, complying with such code," say I with righteous indignation.

"Well, it ain't clean now, and I got no choice but to give you this ticket. Have a nice day."

"The only way I could have a nice day right now is to see you run over by the number 72 bus." I think it was the fifty-dollar fine talking.

"What did you say?"

"Have a nice day as well," I reply.

It's the next morning. I'm in early to tally up last night's figures and make a run to the bank. Temporarily comforted that today can't possibly go as badly as yesterday, I sit and actually enjoy a container of coffee brought in from Milos Restaurant on the corner. Looking through the *Times,* I see an article about Great Britain having elected a female Prime

Minister. Interesting stuff, I think, and something to take my mind off my hapless situation.

My mood changes as I unconsciously pick up the ringing phone, having forgotten to disguise my voice. On the other end is the friendly collection agent for *Fieldcrest Mills*, with whom I've spoken on more than one occasion. I'm informed that the company will be delaying shipments until a payment is received for their invoice now sixty days past due. There is some mention of turning the account over for collection—so what else is new?

"A check will be going out today," I assure the agent. "We've had some problems with our accounting staff, which has since been remedied. My apologies for any inconvenience to you and *Fieldcrest*."

Not too early in the day to begin the lying cycle, I think.

Now I discover the report Lou laid out for me right before his visit was cut short by yesterday's unfortunate events. Math is not my greatest skill, but even I could understand that what is in the report is devastating. The fine owed to the IRS complicates matters even further—if that is even possible. Lou concludes that with Christmas so many months away, the business can only survive for one or two more months.

I come to the conclusion that I am in far over my head. Maybe retailing is not my long suit after all. I go scrambling through the file cabinets in search of our insurance policy. I yank file folder after file folder out of drawers and dump them onto the floor. Finally I discover the manila envelope with the Travelers logo in the bottom of one of the cabinets. I read it over to ensure that on the odd chance these premises are once again struck by Jewish lightning, we will be covered.

I have to be clever about this. How do I make it look like an accident? My pyrotechnic background will not be of any help. Then I remember that short circuit incident we had last year. The lights flickered, then dimmed and finally went out completely, along with the air conditioner. I eventually located the source of the bad wiring in the basement, made a temporary repair and then called an electrician.

What if it were to happen again?

But first, let me gather up the things I do not want to see destroyed—namely the three grand in the safe that was going to get deposited in the bank. I slip the cash into a leather *attaché* case and leave it near the front door. I speedily drop down to the basement and to the very spot that caused last year's problem. After mangling an electrical wire so that it will short circuit, I place a carton of newsprint we use for packing on top of the damaged wire. The smoldering begins to occur, and it's my cue to hit the road.

I race up the stairs, grab the leather bag, open the door and leave without even locking up. I just need to get the hell out of there. The next thing I know I'm standing on the platform of the 72nd Street station of the I.R.T., in full panic mode—having no idea where I'm going next

Chapter 38 • The Voice

"When the whole world is silent, even one voice becomes powerful."

-Malala Yousafzai

My elevator descends at gravity-defying speed. No floor buttons are lit. Don't see an emergency button. The bottom-most light is marked with the letter 'P.'

"Where am I?" I, the sole passenger, ask.

"Let's just say it's your final trip," says *The Voice*.

"What do you mean final trip?"

"I have been warning you about this for quite some time," it replies.

"About what?" I ask, agitatedly.

"Let's start with your opinions on the hereafter."

"You die; you decompose; end of story. Even Mozart decomposed. What other conclusion is possible? And why are we talking about this now?" I ask the invisible presence.

"In a few moments you will understand—and the reason for this conversation will become apparent."

"Hah!"

"Laugh now, but I have reason to know that your smirk will soon become a scowl."

"What do you think you know that I don't?" is my dubious response.

"First, do you realize that last evening you passed beyond this mortal coil?"

"I did what?"

"You keeled over. You kicked the bucket. You bit the dust. You bought the farm. You…"

I thought I was hearing a replay of Monty Python's *Dead Parrot* routine.

"Wait. What are you trying to tell me?"

"Thirty minutes ago, your *attaché* case fell onto the subway tracks, and you were going to jump down from the platform to retrieve it. Is this sounding familiar? I whispered to you, 'Don't do this, Henry.'"

"I'm vaguely recalling it."

"I said, 'Henry, this is not a good idea,' and you replied, 'What could happen? I don't see or hear a train coming.'"

"Please continue," I urge.

"Can you remember anything that happened after that?" *The Voice* asks.

"Wait. I recall the train suddenly bearing down on me. It must have come from beyond the curve in the tracks. I didn't see it until the last minute. Oh, my God! Am I actually dead?"

"Quite," I am assured

"Well, that could alter some of my future plans, a bit, couldn't it?"

"I think your conclusion is on solid ground, even though you are not."

"So what was I so wrong about?" I inquire.

"You said there was no such thing as an afterlife—no heaven and no hell. Now you're going to discover reality to be quite the contrary."

"If that's true, then am I in heaven?"

"No, try again."

"Are you saying that I am in Hell?"

"Take stock on what has been your life. Would you say you led an exemplary one?"

"I wasn't that bad."

"Compared to Himmler, probably not."

"Aren't you being just a tad judgmental? Yes, I've done some things I'm not exactly proud of, but nothing that would earn me a one-way ticket on the *southbound express*. Besides, I don't even believe you. I can't be dead.

Dead means bereft of any sense of physicality," I insist.

"Suppose you describe for me, one physical sensation you are feeling at the moment."

"That's easy. I can hear you," I declare, to my seemingly outwitted opponent.

"You, and only you. What you and I communicate remains in the vault, so to speak. That's because I have been your spirit guide for lo these twenty-nine years. Unfortunately I have been woefully ill equipped for the task.

When I first came on your scene, I knew this would not be a slam-dunk. I even requested a transfer. But, alas, my supervisor had no available replacement, after several thousand qualified spirit guides who knew better, turned down the position.

"Yes, you can hear me," *The Voice* continues, "but not through the aural senses…"

"Oh, come on," I interrupt, defiantly. "You know I don't believe in this crap."

"Have it your way. But you are unprepared to handle what you are about to experience. And I'm only permitted to remain with you a short time longer. Then, you'll be on your own."

I contemplate, deeply, what is being said, but I'm unable to summon any physical sensations. Even my jock itch, a life-long companion, seems to have vanished.

I pinch myself hard, but can feel no pain. No sounds but the whisperings of *The Voice* come to me.

When the armpit sniffing self-test proves negative, I toy with the remote possibility that I could actually be an ex-life form, but stubbornly cling to denial.

"**THIS IS A STUPID DREAM,**" I shout. "I will soon awaken, and everything will be back to normal. Yet, I did jump onto the tracks to fetch my *attaché* case. I do remember the train.

"**Yikes. I'm dead!**"

"Ah, reality sets in," says *The Voice*. "Now you can get on with your, er, afterlife. You see, you have not actually reached Hell—just yet. It is my professional duty to prepare you for the next phase. Just let me know when you are ready to listen—and believe."

"Well, on the off-chance that you just may be right this time, I give you my undevoted attention," says the dead, but still sarcastic, me.

"That's precisely what you have been doing for better than a quarter-century, and is clearly the reason for your current, and let me add, permanent, dilemma."

"Okay, okay. Skip the lecture and get on with it."

"Brace yourself. The phrase *southbound express*, you uttered a while back, was pretty apt. You're plummeting towards Hell at speeds that violate the physical laws of motion. You haven't actually arrived, but when you do, it will be like nothing you've read about nor imagined," warns *The Voice*.

"I won't smolder in an eternal flame while fire licks away at my private parts?"

"Not exactly."

"I won't have to walk around on an ever-burning surface, turning the bottoms of my feet into examples of my mother's roast beef?"

"Not quite."

"No making direct contact with brimstone, whatever that is?"

"Hardly."

"Then just what the hell is Hell?" I query.

"It is a dynamic concept, designed to fit the specific being, applying to no other. Your Hell has its own private signature, if you will. It's custom tailored to your specifications. In fact, applied to others, it mightn't be experienced as Hell, at all."

"If I understand you correctly, you are saying that things that annoyed me in life will now be hurled at me, a million fold, in a never ending stream."

"You are amazingly astute, to grasp this concept so quickly. But hold onto that feeling," says *The Voice*. "We are about to arrive at the last stop."

"Does this mean you will be leaving me?"

"This," said *The Voice*, "is the end of the line…the final destination, sort of."

"Will you at least write?"

"Would that I could. Though you are a complete schmuck, I will miss you. You have brought laughter in a sorrowful world. I'll never forget the time you…"

"Glad I was a good source of entertainment for you," I interrupt. "All that time I thought you were just a voice in my head, to which I gave little credence.

As a matter of fact, the *EST* people advised me to totally ignore you."

"Which is precisely what you did—and why your life has ended so abruptly. And by the way, you'll meet plenty of *EST* people down here, including the founder. Had you listened to me on occasion, you would have enjoyed a great deal of prosperity in a very long life. According to your blueprint, you were designed to live another sixty years. Incidentally, do you remember when you kept bemoaning the fact that you would never inherit anything? Wrong about that, too. In four days, an uncle you surely remember is scheduled to croak, and you're named as his primary beneficiary. I believe he is currently worth close to a billion."

"You son-of-a-bitch. Why tell me this now? I'm not exactly in a position to capitalize on this information, am I?"

"There was much I knew that I wasn't at liberty to divulge. I did, however, attempt to steer you in the right direction. It was your obstinacy that prevented you from taking my counsel. Let's discuss some of that advice, for old time's sake. Remember the sandbox?"

"Ah, the sandbox," I remember, a smile forming to my face.

"You and that moron friend of yours, Teddy, decided to fire a homemade rocket from a launch pad in a sand box."

"Yes, the one in the middle of our housing project."

"If you recall, I specifically reminded you of the inherent danger in using explosives within a densely populated area."

"It was a rocket. It wasn't meant to explode," I offer in defense.

"Talk to the *Challenger* crew about that one. And incidentally, you are not likely to meet any of them where you're going."

"There were no human casualties resulting from our little fiasco," I remind the Voice.

"True, but Rusty the dog experienced a sex change as a consequence."

"He shouldn't have been sniffing around the area."

"Dogs are prone to do that."

"Okay, what else?"

"As long as we're talking about pyrotechnics, your adventure on the *Disorient Express* comes to mind."

"Oh, you are referring to that little motorman's surprise."

"You seemed to have an affinity for explosives."

"No more than most kids."

"No more than most saboteurs," corrects *The Voice*.

"I made some noises as a kid."

"Yes, and what about the time you and your pals reported to the police that you were attacked by a band of crazed Puerto Ricans, and robbed of all your money?"

"We had spent all of our cash on the Coney Island boardwalk, and lied to the cops so that they would put us on the subway."

"But they didn't, did they?"

"Not exactly. Took the cops about three minutes to figure out that we had made the whole thing up.

"That was Sergeant Michael O'Sullivan of the 60th Precinct."

"Yes, good old Sergeant O'Sullivan. Didn't look very bright, but looks can deceive. Son of a bitch called my mother, told her the story, and she suggested that he keep me overnight. I can still hear her voice, loud and clear through the phone's earpiece."

"Now, that was not the first time you aggravated you poor mother."

"No, and certainly not the last. I may have been instrumental in her seeking psychiatric help."

"May have been?" challenges the Voice.

"I was a rotten kid. Always doing things to get her attention, few deserving of a merit badge."

"You were not the darling of your school, either. In fact you were the only kid to get suspended from kindergarten."

"That wasn't my fault."

"Right. Little Ronnie Weinstein should never have had his lower lip where you wanted to swing your fist."

"Ronnie Weinstein: I never liked that little bastard."

"Your mother's school appearances were requested by no less than ten teachers and two principals."

"Those were overreactions, in many cases."

"You also did a bit of writing in your time."

"Yes, the words flowed easily from my pen."

"I'm referring to your affinity for marking up walls in public places. Most people outgrow that when they are past their adolescence, in your case a goal that will remain unachieved."

"My writing was not limited to graffiti."

"Correct. Your tax returns could have earned the *National Book Creative Achievement Award*."

"I took some liberties with certain tax code definitions. We all do that. In fact, if you don't, you pick up the tab for those who do."

"The *IRS* doesn't see it that way. In fact they get a little upset when they discover that a citizen has a propensity for performing pretax prestidigitation."

"Lewisburg would have been the nicest thirty-six months I could ever spend, had Gopher not gotten me off with a fine."

"But a few years before that sad day with Agent Miriam Klenda-Jones, your hand developed uncontrollable urges to counter the natural gravitational pull objects have in their owner's pockets or bags."

"It was a phase."

"Did you enjoy *Bayview Correctional Facility*?"

"As vacations go, not especially."

"So, do you now appreciate how your miscreant behavior has led you to your current situation?

I am unable to come up with a glib reply.

"And now we must part."

"Please don't go. I'm scared," I plead.

"Not my choice, I'm afraid. This is goodbye. Besides, you don't believe in any of this 'crap,' anyway."

"Wait. I don't even know your name."

"My friends call me *Aieoueah*," says *The Voice* as it trails off into nothingness.

"What kind of name is *Aieoueah*? You parents must have had quite a sense of humor. I can just hear the neighborhood kids, 'Can *Aieoueah* come out and play?' '*Aieoueah* stole my lunchbox.'

"Are you still there?" I cry to the now nonexistent *Voice*. "Were you ever really there?"

Silence.

And with that, the 'P' indicator lights up, the door opens and I feel myself being drawn out by some invisible force.

"You can't leave me," I cry, but there is no one to hear, or to sympathize, or even to acknowledge my angst.

Chapter 39 • Final Destination

I don't believe in an afterlife, so I don't have to spend my whole life fearing hell, or fearing heaven even more. For whatever the tortures of hell, I think the boredom of heaven would be even worse.

-Issac Asimov

So here I am, completely alone, trying to imagine what my first hellish experience might be. I venture forth into the abyss, and as I become mired in it, I hear what sounds like a cheap radio, its volume increasing until it is at an ear-shattering level.

It is church music, interspersed with hip-hop, and then the voice of Barry Manilow. It all begins to blend together in a cacophonous soup, and becomes louder and louder.

"Stop! I can't take it any longer. Please…" I scream after just minutes of this auditory torture.

And it stops.

I cannot believe my good fortune. I just have to say the word 'stop' to halt the offending crescendo.

Suddenly a huge TV screen appears before me.

"Don't get tooooo cocky," flash the words. "You will be infuriated at random intervals throughout the day and night. It will be thrust upon you when you least expect or appreciate it. Attempts to block the sound will be fruitless. It will cease as suddenly as it began, but not at your choosing."

Though not especially pleased, I welcome the respite just the same.

I am soon aware of the presence of another being standing beside me. Its approach I didn't detect, but it is definitely here, as its malodorous breath attests.

I try backing away. An invisible wall blocks my movement. The mouth is just inches away. I can recall only one other time when I smelled anything quite like this. It was while I awaited interrogation by the I.R.S. agent. It made my mother's cooking seem almost aromatic by comparison.

"**H**i," says the entity, with a breathy sound and an unwelcome stench. "**H**ow are you? "Name's **H**owie. **H**owie **H**ochstein." The entity's hand is extended in anticipation of a get-acquainted shake. I reluctantly extend mine.

"You look familiar. Have we met before?"

My bile rises. It feels like I'm shaking hands with a cold, wet turd.

"Yes, "**H**ochstein's the name. And ins**h**urance is my game. **H**a, **h**a, **h**a." The stench becomes magnified with the exhaling of each syllable.

I cringe with the thought that Howie Hochstein could be my new companion.

"Look, Howie. I'm new around here, and I've got to look for a place to stay, so if you'll excuse me, I must be off."

"What's your **H**urry, **H**enry?" asks Howie. "Everyone needs ins**h**urance. Why don't you take a moment to read this prop**h**osal? Sign now and qualify for a free gift: A year's subscription to F**h**ishing Magazine, compliments of the **H**artford Group."

"Er, not right now, Howie. Why don't you leave me your business card, and I'll call you when I get settled. 'Kay?"

"You are new here. No need for a business card, or a call. I will be with you c**h**onstantly. I'll be around to answer your ins**h**urance questions whenever you have them. W**h**at could be better than that?"

I long for the return of the dreadful music (which it does) and for Howie to disappear (which he doesn't).

I wonder why the *Spanish Inquisition* never thought of this technique. I know I must think. But for me, thinking is not one of the possibilities, as the combination of Howie's breath and my three least favorite musical genres blend together, assaulting multiple senses simultaneously.

Howie, seeing the panic in my face, tries to soothe me. "I can see your conc**h**ern," says the sympathetic Hochstein. "Sometimes the only thing a fella needs is a little peace of mind. And with **H**artford's budget plan…"

"Enough!" I scream, as my hands clenching tightly around Howie's neck barely cause a ripple in his smooth delivery.

"…in m**h**anageable payments "

I try to compose myself, as I slide down the wall into a sitting position, my eyes bulging. Howie's mouth remains close to my ear, reassuring me, without letup, that everything will be fine, because that is what insurance is all about.

I didn't know how long the torment lasted—only that it had mercifully stopped. "What next?" I utter, fully expecting Howie to provide an insurance answer. Instead, three tall men, shaking their heads at my shame, stand beside me.

The first speaker is thin and gray and wears a clerical collar. "You are here because you have sinned," he says, holding up a bible with one hand and poking a bony finger into my chest. "You have turned an angry face toward the Lord, and He has turned His back on you."

"Sorry, Reverend, wrong religion. **Next**!"

An ugly, toothless man bearing the nametag "*Ayatollah* in Chief " approaches and warns me that Allah has become impatient with me, also poking my chest—nearly puncturing it with his finger .

"Impatient? What's He do when he's really upset?" I ask.

"You don't want to find out," answers the man of the cloth.

"Step aside old man, and make room for the Rabbi," I insist, in a true act of ecumenism.

As the *Ayatollah of Ayatollahs* moves aside, he imparts, "The wrath of Allah is upon you."

"Tell him to get in line," I say, as I motion the Rabbi to come closer.

"Now what poisonous snakes are in your bag, *Reb*?"

"Well, for all practical purposes," says the Rabbi in a sing-song tone, "we don't believe in hell, although we do approve of marriage, which can be similar."

"My sentiments, exactly, Rabbi, and for that reason—not my experience."

"G-d is not pleased with you, young man," repeating the poking actions of the previous admonishers.

"What's with the fingers in the chest? And I'm not exactly thrilled with Him, either. Doesn't fit the nice guy description. Kills babies, permits children to starve, sanctions plagues? And this is just on Tuesdays."

"Blasphemy!" comes the simultaneous cry from the three messengers of God.

"You guys should work as a trio. You're really good."

I think that as long as I'm here, these characters can hold no sway over me. This gives me the confidence to become even more defiant. It's the devil I fear, and for good cause, having recently run into one of his representatives in the insurance business.

The defeated clerics fade into the mist as quickly as they arrived, leaving me temporarily alone. This doesn't last, as I now find myself in a subway car, crowded with most the frustrating types I encountered in life.

Next to me is a young black man, holding a boom box the size of a *Sub-Zero*. From it comes language that would have made Lenny Bruce blush, filling the air with angry, racist, cop-hating, misogynistic messages. And as an accompaniment, the PA system occasionally chimes in, producing announcements that no passenger can comprehend, at a decibel level sufficient to crumble the polar icecaps.

A parade of homeless men enters from the connecting car, leaving the door open, allowing screaming wheels against rickety track to bombard my senses as the train whizzes through the curved tunnel.

"My name's Jerome," shouts the first one. "I just got out of prison after eight years for a crime I do not remember committing. I am homeless and hungry. If you could spare a quarter, nickel, dime, even a penny, it would be appreciated."

I decide to be charitable, and pull a penny out of my pocket. "Here," I say, placing the coin in Jerome's hand. "Don't spend it all in one place."

"Thank you, and may God bless you," Jerome tells me, before realizing that he has just exchanged a blessing for a unit of currency that could not buy even a Chiclet from a subway gum dispenser. "What am I supposed to do with a Goddamn penny?"

"Then take it out of your spiel," say I, looking up with a saccharine smile.

A seemingly endless horde stampedes from the car behind, each victim repeating a variation of the previous monetary appeal, with no relief in sight.

The car soon fills with a myriad of conversations conducted in Korean, Hindi, Mandarin, French Creole, Russian, Spanish, Farsi, Swahili, Urdu and Uzbek, throughout the car. Every passenger talks simultaneously, re-sembling a Mah Jong evening at my mother's apartment, in this rolling *Tower of Babel*.

"Doesn't anyone speak English, anymore?" I ask, to no one in partic-ular.

The answer comes from the little man on my right, who I promptly rec-ognize as Howie Hochstein. "Have you had a chance to conshider the policy I designed for your specifhic needs?"

At this, I release a tirade of epithets heavily embedded with Anglo-Sax-on modifiers.

"Now, why hurl insults at me? I'm only looking out for hyour prothec-tion. In these horrifying and threatening times, no one should be without life inshurance."

"Has it occurred to you that since I am already dead, my need for insur-ance is significantly reduced? Have you sold even a single policy since your arrival?"

"Come to think of, it no. I wondered if I was losing my touch," Howie replies. "Whell, I'm not going to let a little challenge like that dishsuade me. I'll just have to become more aggrhessive."

My attention is soon arrested by a man whose clothing is festooned with large religion-themed buttons—too numerous to count. He begins to re-cite, borrowing from the text on those buttons. "Jesus is coming, Jesus is coming. Jesus is our savior…"

A black man extols the virtues of the strict Muslim life. "Allah is in all of us, black man, white man, brown man, yellow man, red man…" quitting when he runs out of colors. "Let Allah fill your heart with his everlasting love."

I have trouble recalling many Native American devotees to Islam.

Spokesmen for their chosen faiths spew their rhetoric, occasionally drowning out one another. I hope the lot of them will eventually get upset enough to kill their competition. I expect these to be joined by a Jew selling his own line of dogma, but then gratefully remember that Jews do not proselytize.

That myth is quickly dispelled by a group of three in their early twenties wearing *Jews for Jesus* sweatshirts. "Read about *Jews for Jesus*," they shout, passing pamphlets to any who would accept them, and dirty looks to those who would not.

When an attempt is made to hand me one, I hold up my hand and say, "Sorry, I'm already a member of *Goys for Moses*, and I sometimes attend meetings at *Hindus for Mohammed*."

The parade continues. Something resembling a human, but only barely, sashays by. Half his head sports a crew cut dyed in a palette of colors, ranging from a deep purple to an acid green. The other half is like a bowling ball, holes and all. This fellow has more piercings than Richard III after the battle of Bosworth Field.

"Gays in the military: Ask! Tell!" cries a person whose gender could not be immediately identified. "Gays in the Saint Patrick's Day parade: what are they afraid of? Pederasts in the priesthood...? Oh, sorry—done that."

He leaves suddenly when Howie tries to sell him a straight life policy.

The train comes to a sudden stop in the midst of a tunnel. I wait for the inevitable cry from the PA system that would make some barely recognizable apology for the inconvenience. Instead, it is the Voice of Kate Smith singing "God Bless America," loud enough to cause a Himalayan avalanche. It almost drowns out a Chinese couple's conversation. Hochstein adjusts his vocal timbre as to not be over shouted.

To pass the time while waiting for the journey to resume, I try reading. All that is available is Awake Magazine, left on my lap by a wandering *Witness of Jehovah*; the latest International Cribbage Championship scores and a pamphlet showing a picture of a smiling elderly Nun talking an Indian woman out of using birth control—not exactly a plethora of great reading material.

It is then that I look up at one of the marquees located throughout the car. On a black background and written in large white block letters, is posted the name of the line (666), route (Via Purgatory) and final destination (Hell):

The heat in the car is enough to toast marshmallows. Attempts to move are frustrated by huge wads of chewing gum that anchor feet to floor.

Kate Smith is replaced by Billy Graham, and then by Jim and Tammy Faye Bakker. They are soon followed by Pat Robertson. Although some of these folks are not yet dead, I'm confident that this will be their ultimate destination. Their speeches focus on sin, more sin, and would you believe it, still more sin? It makes me think about the Roman Catholic Bishop of the Philippines, whose name just happens to be *Cardinal Sin*. That brings a smile to my otherwise angry lips.

I begin to realize that this customized Hell is not having its intended effect. But the demonic force responsible for this design is also getting the message; the plan is not working. I crave misery, and can't be happy without it.

I am subjected to virtually every torture that daunted me for my entire my life, only at a highly accelerated rate. And I'm loving it—hardly Hell, at all. And that's when it happens. The noise ceases. Howie Hochstein keels over with a heart attack brought on by prolonged ball breaking. A nun, who had earlier pointed a finger at me while incessantly shaking her head 'no,' slumps down in her seat, tongue dangling, as a hefty bundle of *Hustler* magazines falls out of her bag onto the floor.

The car's temperature becomes as comfortable as I have ever experienced. A man with the dimensions of the *USS Enterprise*, who has been blocking the door, tears from his neck a gold cross, heavy enough to give the *Grand Inquisitor* a hernia, throws it to the floor as he moves into the train.

The ghetto blaster guy apologizes to every passenger that still has his or her hearing intact for playing such insulting trash, and inserts a *Beethoven's Greatest Hits* cassette in its place. He asks his fellow passengers if the volume is satisfactory.

A voice on the PA, with perfect diction, begs for the forgiveness of all aboard for the inexcusable delay. "Please hold on, passengers," says the crystal clear voice. "The train is starting to move, and we want everyone to be safe."

The Chinese couple finds two seats together and speak in a whisper, inaudible to their fellow passengers.

A headline from the *Daily News* reads:

Thirteen Televangelists Die in Fire
While Engaging in Wild Sex Orgy
Police investigate why stacks
of bibles blocked all exits.

I look all around me, waiting for the next bomb to drop. This seems way too good to be true. I know it can't last, and I prepare myself for any horrific event that is sure to occur. Yes, they'll be back before too long, I think, the priests, the connivers and screamers—the cretins dripping mustard on car seats. The public address system will resume shutting the gates of mercy on its captive audience.

After several serene minutes, I begin to worry. Why are people behaving civilly? Why is my seat suddenly so comfortable? How perfectly I fit in it, with its adjustable lumbar support and tiny footrest. I am just far enough from the adjacent passenger. The gum under my shoe—gone! Had I imagined it?

No horrific events unfold, about which to bitch and moan. The peace that fills the subway car seems to be shared by all aboard, with me the only exception. For the first time since this journey began, I feel uncomfortable, though not with my physical surroundings, as they are still perfect. Somehow the possibility that nothing will ever upset me again is too painful to abide.

I ponder the idea of never uttering another complaint, no one at whom an aspersion can be cast, no air horns blasting at three in the morning, no sanitation workers dropping trashcans seemingly from the tops of buildings to roust me from my sleep, no piles of excrement or empty glass bottles on the subways steps, no cops sleeping in their police cars on the city clock, no *New York Post* headlines, no Donald Trump building monuments to perpetual shade, no pregnant women smoking while holding their own toddlers, no taxicabs with just enough legroom to accommodate a chopstick, no commercials in movie theaters after patrons forked up over five bucks for admission, no subway passengers loudly and proudly discussing their colonoscopies, no department store sales clerks pretending you are not there.

What would it be like to never get pissed off?

The train stops smoothly and the sound of well-oiled doors hiss open.

Then, the announcement can be heard. "Last stop: All passengers please exit. This is…."

The End

Acknowledgements

A salute to my long-deceased parents
who did not disown me, despite my
many acts of juvenile delinquency, and
their struggle to put food on the table.

I especially would have liked
my father to know how I finally
learned to appreciate his tolerance,
and love of nature and history.

—And thanks, Mom, for your sense
of humor — a requirement for survival.

Finally, I'd like to thank those members
of the **Humanists of Sarasota Bay
Writers' Group** for their fine
suggestions on how to improve this work.
Maybe, next time, I'll listen.

About the Author

Barry Zack was born and raised in Brooklyn, New York, much like the main character in the story. His experiences growing up in a working class neighborhoods provided him many survival skills and a hunger to succeed.

His lack of a college degree did not prevent him from achieving success in the business world. He re-invented himself many times in order to survive and prosper.

In addition to writing, Barry keeps himself busy with website and newsletter design and production. He is active in both his Humanist group and with the Environmental Movement.

His blogs can be seen at:
restlessknights.wordpress.com and Sick and Tired of Being Sick and Tired at
http://stobst.blogspot.com.

His environmental website is:
http://ourneighborhoodearth.org.